GRACE SO
AMAZING

GRACE SO AMAZING

Emma-Jeanne Bartlett

BROADMAN PRESS
Nashville, Tennessee

© Copyright 1989 • Broadman Press
All Rights Reserved
4272-33
ISBN: 0-8054-7233-9
Dewey Decimal Classification: B
Subject Heading: Bartlett, Gene // Church Music
Library of Congress Catalog Number: 88-29313
Printed in the United States of America

Unless otherwise stated, all Scripture quotations
are from the King James Version of the Bible.
Scripture quotations marked RSV are from the
Revised Standard Version of the Bible,
copyright 1946, 1952, © 1971, 1973.
Scripture quotations marked NASB are from the
New American Standard Bible. Copyright © The Lockman
Foundation, 1960, 1962, 1963, 1968, 1971, 1972,
1973, 1975, 1977. Used by permission.

Library of Congress Cataloging-in-Publication Data

Bartlett, Emma-Jeanne, 1920-
    Grace so amazing / Emma-Jeanne Bartlett.
      p.   cm.
    ISBN 0-8054-7233-9 : $3.25
    1. Bartlett, Gene, d. 1988.   2. Church musicians—United States—
—Biography.   I. Title.
ML422.B24B37 1989
264'.0613202'092—dc19
    [B]   88-29313
                                                              CIP
                                                              MN

———

To Gene, without whom God's
Grace So Amazing
would not have touched so many lives;
To our children—Larry, Frances, and Reggie;
and to our grandchildren—
Julie, Chris, Scott, Devin, and Nicholas.
I say with Paul, "I thank my God for every
remembrance of you" (Phil 1:3).

CONTENTS

Foreword

Grace So Amazing is the story of an ordinary man made extraordinary in Jesus Christ. Whether directing huge congregations gathered in an open-air tabernacle in singing their favorite gospel songs or in composing music that will certainly be sung in the twenty-first century, Gene Bartlett demonstrated the uncommon gift of staying in touch with people. Perhaps it is the honesty revealed in Gene's music to which people have responded.

Gene's music and his life stand as a testimony to the truth that in happiness or in sorrow God's grace really is enough. When Gene wrote "God's Grace Is Enough For Me," he expressed the heartfelt concerns of many people regarding life's sorrows. Gene's strong affirmation of faith, "that God never promised a day without sorrows . . . but God's grace is enough for me," has comforted many hurting people.

It is rather ironic and surely providential that so much of Gene's music is concerned with how to face the hard realities of life. Gene faced, for more than thirteen years, one of the hardest of those realities called Parkinson's Disease. This debilitating illness took much from Gene and tragically it took his ability to write music, but during these years with a steadfast wife at his side, faith became their song.

Do not be misled into thinking this book is concerned only with the sorrow in the life of Gene and Emma-Jeanne Bartlett. They have known many of life's joys together.

Whether involved in Oklahoma Baptists' Falls Creek Baptist Assembly, sharing a freezer of homemade ice cream with friends, or listening to their granddaughter sing her first solo, they have found great happiness along the way.

Emma-Jeanne has truly been a loyal partner with Gene in life and ministry. She has been there to share the joy and endure the pain, and through it all she has been a source of strength and stability. It is exceedingly fitting that she should be the one to pen this testimony of faith.

It has been my personal blessing to have been touched by the life of Gene Bartlett. As a teenager at Falls Creek, I heard for the first time the call of God while singing "Wherever He Leads I'll Go" under the direction of Gene Bartlett. I was influenced by the homespun Bartlett wisdom in countless conversations. Finally, my life was enriched by the experience of serving as the Bartletts' pastor at Trinity Baptist Church in Oklahoma City. It has been my joy to observe for more than thirty years in the life of Gene Bartlett, God's *Grace So Amazing*.

Several weeks after the words above were written, early on Sunday morning July 10, 1988, Gene passed from this life to life with the Heavenly Father. His two sons Larry and Reggie were by his side for that last earthly moment. On Tuesday morning the family and friends gathered at the grave side. That afternoon they came to Trinity Baptist Church for a memorial service.

It was the kind of service that Gene liked. He had planned and led services very similar many times over the years. It was a time for prayer led by local pastors Steve Graham and Dale Suel. It was a time for remembering led by longtime pastor friends Ben Mosley and Robert Scales. It was a time for the reading of many of Gene's favorite Scripture passages by beloved associate and friend Mary June Tabor. It was a time for music sung by the congregation, Gayle Lowell, Bar-

bara Bell, Bill Benson, and, of course, the Singing Church-men of Oklahoma. The music was led by partners in ministry William J. Reynolds and James Woodward.

Those who knew Gene best were confident the service was just as Gene wanted. The last hymn—"Victory In Jesus"—was a masterful blend of the past, present, and future. Of course, it was the hymn that Gene's dad E. M. Bartlett had written in 1939 and Gene had introduced and made famous among Southern Baptists. The hymn was directed by Gene's son Larry. The Singing Churchmen sang a verse. Larry sang a verse and Gene's granddaughter Julie sang the last verse,

> I heard about a mansion he has built for me in glory,
> And I heard about the streets of gold beyond the
>   crystal sea;
> About the angels singing, and the old redemption
>   story,
> And some sweet day I'll sing up there the song of
>   victory.

With a strikingly clear soprano voice Julie sang without any tears, because she knew her grandfather was indeed experiencing that which she was singing.

We who knew and loved Gene Bartlett will miss him greatly. However, we would not for a second take him from his new life. For as long as we live we will sing his songs. We will pause to remember "Uncle Gene" and we will be grateful to our Lord.

Gary Cook
Nashville, Tennessee

Acknowledgments

I want this book to reflect God's goodness and grace in the life of our family, and particularly in the life of Gene Bartlett, my late husband. I want to show how God can take a very ordinary person and cause good things to take place in his life. Most of all, I want you to see how Christ lived in Gene.

One of Gene's favorite Scriptures was Philippians 1:20-21,

> . . . that in nothing I shall be ashamed, but that with all boldness, as always, so now also Christ shall be magnified in my body, whether it be by life, or by death. For to me to live is Christ, and to die is gain.

I could not have written this book without the help of so many people, and I am most grateful. I thank Connie and Tanya Hay for typing the first draft. Their encouragement was wonderful. My thanks also go to Linda Lawson for thinking I could write the book and for her editorial expertise; to John Gardner for his suggestions, and to Dr. Gary Cook for believing in the value of the book for Southern Baptists.

I am also grateful for dates and clippings from Mary June Tabor, Gene's secretary for twenty-six years, and my friend. She knew exactly the articles and materials I needed.

Dr. Robert S. Scales, a dear friend and colleague, also provided much information. His folder on Gene Bartlett was well organized and very helpful.

Of course, I would never have completed the book without my husband and his unfaltering belief in my ability to tell his story. My children and grandchildren were also very supportive. They kept saying, "You can do it, Mom! You can do it, Nana!"

I could not have written a word without God's help. Even His nudgings in the middle of the night were welcome.

—Emma-Jeanne Bartlett

PART I

GRACE SO AMAZING

Grace so amazing
is with me each day
For this great love
I can never repay.

(Top) The only family picture the E. M. Bartletts ever had made: (left to right) Charles, Joan Tatum Bartlett, Eugene Monroe (E. M.) Bartlett, Sr., and Eugene Monroe, Jr. (Gene) . . . (Bottom) Bartlett, Sr., and Music Publisher Albert E. Brumley (right).

1

Living in a Nightmare

Gene Bartlett, or "Uncle Gene" as he was affectionately known to thousands, wrote the song, "Grace So Amazing," in 1969 as a gift for a friend, evangelistic singer Beverly Terrell. She had often told him she wished there was a song with the message of "Amazing Grace" written within soprano range.

"Grace So Amazing" is not only a gift for a friend, it is also a testimony of the life of Gene Bartlett. God's grace was the sustaining force throughout Gene's life—while growing up in Arkansas, following in his father's footsteps in gospel music, serving as a minister of music, touching the lives of thousands of young people through Falls Creek Baptist Assembly, and helping Oklahoma churches strengthen their music programs as a means of sharing the gospel of Christ.

At no time has the grace of God been more evident than on the journey that began in the summer of 1975 and ended in 1988 as this book was being prepared for the typesetter. The lab reports had been read, the CAT scan had been interpreted, and the doctors had concluded, "Gene, you have Parkinson's disease. It is not life threatening. It can be controlled with medication, but there is no cure."

In June of that year Gene and I had taken a vacation, the first when we did not have some conference or meeting to attend. We were going to get a jump on the expected mobs who in 1976 would crowd into Williamsburg and other areas where our country had its beginnings. Everyone would be going to these places for the bicentennial celebration, and we wanted to avoid the crowds.

One night when we had left our hotel to walk in a nearby shopping center, I noticed Gene was dragging his right leg. We decided it was nothing. He was simply tired from riding and driving that day, so we dismissed it from our minds and enjoyed the rest of the trip.

Upon returning to Oklahoma City he was caught up in the final preparations for five weeks at Falls Creek Baptist Assembly, and his health was not discussed.

In July the assembly began. Gene seemed to become tired more easily than usual, but he never complained, and I didn't say anything. I think I really knew something was wrong, but I tried to ignore the signs. I rationalized that five weeks of leading the music for two worship services each day would make anyone slow down.

As the assembly drew to a close that summer, Gene began to use his right arm less and less. When he directed the music it seemed to be a major effort just to beat the time. We didn't talk about it.

When the assembly ended in August Gene made an appointment to see his doctor. A thorough examination was not done at that time, but the doctor discovered some arthritis and prescribed medication. Gene continued to work, but his right side was getting worse.

I finally concluded that he must have had a stroke. I begged him to see a second doctor. He agreed, and he made an appointment to see an internist. We looked forward to finding out something, believing we could better deal with the situation if we knew for sure what was wrong. After Gene saw the doctor in the middle of October, two neurologists were called in for consultation.

I will never forget the day we received the diagnosis. Neither of us knew anything about Parkinson's. Wasn't that the disease where the patient had uncontrollable tremors? Yet Gene didn't shake very much.

He was put on medication, and we began to read all we could find on Parkinson's disease. One of the first facts we learned was that no two people are affected the same way. We also learned to expect side effects from the medicine.

At first, the medication seemed worse than the disease. It made Gene so sick that when he sang for a funeral or led singing for a meeting he would have to lie down between numbers. Gradually, he became able to tolerate the medicine, and for some three years he continued in his job as director of the Church Music Department for the Baptist General Convention of Oklahoma.

At the time of the diagnosis, Gene had asked me to be sure and tell him when I felt it was time for him to step down. I knew I would not have to do that. He would be aware when he could no longer give his best to Oklahoma Baptists. God had led him this far, and He would surely make it known when to resign.

For weeks after the diagnosis, I felt as though we were living in a nightmare. Surely we would awaken from it and life would return to the way it was before Parkinson's. But that did not happen, and we began to look for the right dosage of medicines.

Throughout the symptoms, the diagnosis, the sickness from the medication, and the moving forward into an increasingly uncertain future, Gene never lost his belief that God was in control. I must admit that at times my faith wavered, but in those times the person who helped me most was Gene himself.

At first only his right side was affected by the disease. Because he was left-handed, Gene pointed to this as a sign of God's goodness. When his speech and movements became slower, he reminded me that he had always been slow talking and moving. People had joked about his "rapid-fire delivery" for years. Gene used to joke that he had to tell people when he was excited.

Gene also pointed to people we encountered along the way as evidence that God was continuing to touch our lives.

One day we were in the neurology department of Oklahoma Memorial Hospital for some tests. As they finished the brain scan that day, the young man operating the scanner confided, "Uncle Gene, you don't know me, but I was saved at Falls Creek one summer while you were leading the invitation hymn."

Gene was first nicknamed "Uncle Gene" by the youth at Trinity Baptist Church in Oklahoma City. It caught on and was picked up by the thousands of youth he encountered during the twenty-six years he directed the music for Falls Creek Assembly. Those young people are adults now, but he is still remembered as "Uncle Gene" to thousands across the Southern Baptist Convention.

That day, in the midst of concern and confusion, God used that young man to reaffirm that our times are indeed in His hands. God showed us yet again His "grace so amazing."

2

Hartford (*Arkansas, That Is*)

In the rugged foothills of the Sugar Loaf, Magazine, and Poteau Mountains in Northwestern Arkansas nestles the little coal-mining town of Hartford.

During the summer of 1918 the Bartlett family moved there from Greenwood, eighteen miles away. Earlier in the year, on a beautiful spring morning in May, a son had been born to Eugene Monroe and Joan Tatum Bartlett, their first child. The parents were overjoyed. They had a son to be named for his father. So the child became Eugene Monroe Bartlett, Jr.

Gene Bartlett, Sr. was an evangelistic singer and teacher of singing schools. However, he had moved to Hartford to establish a music publishing company. The firm would publish paperback songbooks to be used in singing conventions and by gospel quartets. The company, to be known as the Hartford Music Company, was established in 1919 and is still in existence. In later years it was bought by Albert E. Brumley and Sons and now is located in Powell, Missouri.

The Bartlett family were Southern Baptists and became active in the First Baptist Church of Hartford. Gene Bartlett, Sr. served as a deacon. Baptist heritage was an important part of the family. Mrs. Bartlett's father was Reverend John E. Tatum, a Baptist preacher.

Three years after the Bartletts moved to Hartford another son, Charles Scott, was born. This completed their family.

Since Mr. Bartlett was known to his friends and family as Gene, to avoid calling their eldest son Junior, they called him E. M. His family still calls him by that name. Today when the telephone rings and someone asks to speak to E. M., I know immediately that it is either family or someone from Hartford.

Hartford was a good place for a little boy to grow up. There were lots of places to run and play, plenty of fresh air and sunshine. But in spite of this, E. M. was plagued by asthma. However, he did not allow respiratory problems to slow him down very much. He was a typical boy, often causing trouble or was nearby when trouble happened. It was often heard in Hartford, "If that kid of Bart's stays out of jail, it will be a miracle."

E. M. liked to play what he called "jokes" on his little brother and others. Once as they were playing in a piano crate behind the music company, E. M. put Charles Scott in the crate, turned it so the opening was on top, and ran away. Sometime later a passerby heard Charles' screams and got him out.

Another time E. M.'s best friend, Clarvel Beavers, grew tired of playing and fell asleep in his front yard. Seeing him asleep, E. M. meant to pull a prank and dropped a rock on his friend's head. Clarvel was not seriously injured, but E. M. could not sit comfortably for several days. Sometimes the incidents were unintentional, but the little boy had a hard time convincing the adults of this.

Hartford was surrounded by abandoned coal mines. The pits left after the coal had been stripped made delightful places for boys to play—dirty but delightful. These became favorite places for the children of Hartford.

Living near the Bartletts at this time was Mrs. Reed, a teacher in the public schools. One fall a new color was being seen in clothes and accessories. The color was "American Beauty", a pretty, rosy red. Mrs. Reed liked the color and had spent most of a Saturday morning dyeing several pieces of clothing. She had just finished hanging them on a clothes-line in her yard when E. M. came by, taking a shortcut to his home for lunch. He had spent the morning playing in the pits. He must have been fascinated by seeing so much of one color all in a row. He proceeded to go down the line, placing his coal-soiled handprints on each piece. Mrs. Bartlett was so humiliated that she helped Mrs. Reed remove the color and the dirt and re-dye everything that Saturday afternoon. Only later were they able to laugh about the Saturday they spent *dying*.

The first cold spell of the fall was celebrated as "hog-killing time." Neighbors pitched in to help each other, and in turn received help when their hogs were ready to be butchered. They also shared the fresh meat with one another. Many times the Bartletts would come home to find a stick of sa-lami, a ham, or some sausage on the kitchen table.

The fat trimmings and scraps from the hogs were used to make lard. The scraps were boiled in a black wash pot over an open fire in the yard. The pot was the same one used for heating water and boiling clothes on wash day. The lard was used to season and cook food and usually lasted a family from one hog killing to the next. On one of these lard-cooking occasions, E. M. saw a long limb sticking from under the black pot. Without considering the consequences he jumped on the end of the limb, turning the entire kettle of boiling lard over. Fortunately, no one was burned.

You may be sure the neighbors knew something was bound to happen when "Bart's boy" came around.

3

A Rotten Egg in the Classroom

When E. M. started to school, he began twelve years characterized by ups and downs in his education. His belief that it was more fun to play than to study showed in both his grades and his behavior.

For example, he recalled finding a rotten egg on the way to school one morning. Arriving in his classroom before anyone else, he threw the egg into the cloakroom. The odor was so terrible the teacher had to move the students to another location until their room could be cleaned and deodorized. Luckily for E. M., the teacher never found out who threw the egg.

Summers were fun and lazy in the foothills of the mountains. Days seemed made for a game of sandlot baseball in a nearby pasture. Hartford played against other communities with such colorful names as Frog Town, Prairie Creek, and Shiloh.

Hartford's arch rival was Bolin Camp, a community just outside town. The two teams were enemies, and their games always ended in a fight. On the Hartford team were several Italian-American boys who could take care of themselves in a fight. E. M., by his own admission, never won a fight but enjoyed the protection of his Italian teammates because in winning they made him look good.

Another favorite activity on a hot, muggy summer day was to sneak off and go "skinny dipping." James Fork Creek which ran through town and the "Old Pump Hole" were the scenes of many happy times. Sometimes the swimming took precedence over chores to be done, and then the swimming holes were made off limits by the parents.

E. M. had a large number of cousins living in the Fort Smith area, and each summer they would come to visit. These were especially fun times. In turn E. M. would spend two weeks with them in Fort Smith. Selling watermelons on Rye Hill and going to the circus were two favorite activities.

There were sports for each season of the year in Hartford. The teams were usually made up of kids who attended the same church. One fall First Baptist Church had a football team. Knowing that some of the boys who attended the Catholic Church were good players, E. M. recruited them to play football with First Baptist. To be eligible to play they had to attend Sunday School at the Baptist church. The boys came, the team won, and all went well until the priest found that the Catholic boys were going to Sunday School at the Baptist church. The next Sunday morning he was standing on the street corner directing his boys back to their own church.

4

First Steps on the King's Road

E. M. was always taken to church by his parents. It was understood that he would sit on the front pew with his father sitting directly behind him. Even with this close supervision, E. M. naturally managed to get into mischief from time to time.

Mr. Bartlett gave the boys ten cents each for the offering on Sundays. They were allowed to walk to the church and passed through town on their way. For a time one of the stores had a slot machine. On one occasion, E. M. took five cents of his offering and put it into the machine. To his amazement he hit the jackpot and it seemed like money went everywhere. He was so scared he left the money and ran on to the church. The Lord only got a nickel that day, but you can be sure he never tried the slot machine again. He knew he could never explain that much money to his dad.

E. M. had been in Sunday School and church all of his life, so it was only natural that he would come to know Jesus as his personal Savior. This happened during a revival meeting when he was eleven years old. The pastor, Ford F. Gantt, was preaching.

Five or six boys always sat together and E. M. was the first to move into the aisle during the invitation. Upon reaching the pastor he realized his buddies were right behind him.

While E. M.'s parents had provided a Christian home for him, he credited his favorite Sunday School teacher with helping him to realize his need for Christ in his life. This teacher was Mrs. John Griffith, the mother of Inez Scales (Mrs. Robert S. Scales). E. M. pays tribute to Mrs. Griffith by saying she was very knowledgable about the Word of God and also loved young boys. She reached out and touched these boys, claiming them for Jesus Christ. The amazing grace of God was evident even in the early years of E. M. Bartlett as God raised up people to influence him in ways that would last a lifetime.

5

First Notes of a Lifelong Song

During his high school years, E. M. helped in his Father's music publishing company before and after school. He also traveled over the area, singing in gospel quartets.

Twice each year, in January and June, Hartford Music Company conducted "singing normals" which lasted three weeks each session. Some of these were held in Hartford and others in Fort Smith. There was only one small hotel in Hartford so friends and neighbors opened their homes to the more than three hundred people from Western Arkansas and Eastern Oklahoma who came to study.

Outstanding personalities were brought in to help teach music. As a high school senior, E. M. was allowed to miss school in January and again in June to study under such great men as Will H. and J. H. Ruebush and Homer Rodeheaver.

The Ruebush brothers were founders of the Shenandoah Conservatory of Music in Dayton, Virginia. Mr. Rodeheaver was the evangelistic singer for Billy Sunday. (For you younger people who might not know these names, they are the equivalent of Billy Graham and George Beverly Shea.)

E. M. said of his senior year at Hartford High, "I just squeaked through with a low-C average." While he had gained valuable knowledge about music and much inspiration from the superb teachers in the singing schools, missing six weeks from one semester took its toll on his grades.

As with most young people of his time, no particular direction for his life had taken shape. He only felt it would be in music. Before the Ruebushes returned to Virginia, they invited E. M. to come there to attend the conservatory.

After he graduated from high school in the spring, the fall of 1934 found father and son on their way to launch E. M.'s college career. It was the depth of the Depression and money was scarce. However, the school had offered a work scholarship and, believing God was leading in that direction, they began the long, hard drive of more than a thousand miles in a Model-A Ford. To save money, they spent most nights with friends along the way. It was a good time of fellowship and camaraderie between father and son.

One change made as he began his college education was that E. M. became known as "Gene." So from this point I will refer to him as Gene.

On the way to Shenandoah Conservatory, Gene and his father stopped in Nashville, Tennessee. There the elder Bartlett sold the publishing rights—to the National Baptist Publishing Board—to enough songs to pay Gene's tuition. "If you ever hear black people sing 'Just a Little While to Stay Here' or 'Everybody Will Be Happy Over There,' just remember those songs paid for my first semester's tuition," Gene used to recall.

Upon arriving in the beautiful Shenandoah Valley of Virginia they found the Shenandoah Conservatory of Music at Dayton which had been established and was operated by the United Brethren denomination. It was the typical religious school with compulsory chapel attendance each day.

The school maintained a certain dignity indigenous to the area. Coat and tie were required dress for the dining hall at every meal. Since money was scarce in 1934, and in order to have more for fun and dates, Gene spent his laundry money on girls and did his own shirts. He has confessed that only the collars, cuffs, and fronts of the shirts were ironed. "Why do the whole shirt?" he asked. "I ironed all that could be seen!"

Since money was in such short supply during these years, Gene was able to come home only once a year during the Christmas holidays. Gene recalled that the entire city of Hartford came out to meet the train when he arrived. "Of course, they met the train every day, just to see who would get off!" he laughed.

For the next two years Gene studied music, music theory, piano, composition, and voice in the area of the country which has been called the "Cradle of Shaped-Note Singing in America." He learned of the fabulous heritage of the music which is unique to the United States.

However, school was not all work and no play. Fourteen inches of snow one winter found him enjoying his first bob-sledding.

Gene's first trip to a honky-tonk was short-lived because he kept remembering an admonition from his parents that a good name was important. He recognized that surely this behavior did not contribute to a good name.

Gene does not admit to taking part in a prank in which the conservatory president's small British-made sports car (the smallest car made at that time) was put into his office.

Gene fulfilled the requirements of his work scholarship by stoking the furnace in the boys' dorm, sweeping the music building, and traveling with a quartet. They sang in West Virginia and Pennsylvania, promoting the college.

Gene played saxophone with the college symphony. The fact that his girl friend also played was, no doubt, an incentive. He spent his time trying to convince her to give up the bass fiddle for a piccolo since it fell to his lot to carry the instrument to and from performances.

After graduation from Shenandoah Music School, there was as yet no definite direction to Gene's life. He still entertained the dream of doing something in music. But what?

When asked what kind of music he would pursue, Gene would reply, "I don't know exactly, but it will be music that glorifies the name of the Lord."

(Top) The Gospel quartet Gene traveled with in Arkansas, Oklahoma, and Texas: (left to right) Gene Bartlett, second tenor; Jeff Duncan, first tenor; Deacon Utley, baritone; Lynn Utley, pianist; Huey Biggs, bass. (Middle) Gene, Emma-Jeanne, Larry, and Fran when they were at Central Baptist Church in Muskogee, Oklahoma. (Bottom) Gene home on leave with Larry and Fran.

PART II

LIVE
YOUR
SONG

Grace all sufficient
though sinful I've been,
God loved me so much
in spite of my sin.

(Top) Here Gene (at mike), Dr. T. B. Lackey, and Dr. Joe Ingram broke ground for the B. B. McKinney Music Chapel at Falls Creek. (Middle) Gene, Dr. W. Hines Sims, and Mrs. B. B. McKinney when Sims was honored on his twentieth anniversary as secretary of the Church Music Department, BSSB. (Bottom) Reggie and Fran Bartlett at Falls Creek.

1

Beowulf and Stamps-Baxter

Just after Gene received his diploma from the Shenandoah Conservatory of Music in the spring of 1936, Mr. Bartlett sold the Hartford Music Co. to his partner, John A. McClung, and joined the Stamps-Baxter Music Co. of Dallas, Texas. Gene moved there with his family.

This was a busy time. Among other things, Gene sang in the Stamps-Baxter Quartet, traveling and promoting the sale of songbooks. The quartet had a 6 AM radio broadcast each weekday from the Hotel Adolphus. Many times they completed a singing engagement and then traveled all night, going directly to the hotel to be on time for the early-morning broadcast.

The continuation of Gene's formal education had been postponed with the move to Dallas. However, he enrolled for the second semester at Southern Methodist University. His major was to be English literature. The only course he ever admits flunking was *Beowulf*.

Gene was majoring in literature rather than music in part because Mr. Bartlett believed that every person, regardless of his profession, should have a liberal-arts degree. Perhaps his own five degrees, including a Bachelor of Oratory, explain this philosophy. His family had a great deal of fun with Mr. Bartlett's B.O. degree, especially when he occasionally became a little boastful about his education.

During this period Gene lived a grueling schedule. He attended classes each morning and spent the afternoons working as the chief mail clerk at Stamps-Baxter. In addition, he continued to sing with the quartet, travel to concerts, and make early morning broadcasts.

Besides handling the mailing of all music publications, Gene's staff mailed fifteen-minute recordings which were used in daily radio broadcasts over a great part of the United States and Mexico. Records were very different in those days. They were large fifteen-inch records which contained fifteen minutes of singing by the Stamps Quartet which included V. O. Stamps, one of the founders of the company.

The broadcasts were aired over station KRLD in Dallas which was not too strong during the day but at night was boosted to fifty-thousand watts. This enabled the station to reach a vast area of the country.

About this same time, the first "all-night singing" was held in the Cotton Bowl in Dallas. At this singing, a songbook, *Favorite Radio Songs*, was offered to those who would send one dollar. More than forty-one thousand requests came in, and Gene and the mail crew sent out about a thousand books per day.

As part of his work with the publishing company, Gene's father was teaching singing schools around the country. At a school in Tulsa, Oklahoma, he suffered a stroke. He was staying in the home of Marvin Dalton whose friend and roommate, Cedric Weehunt, a regular on the old "Lum and Abner" radio show, is credited with saving Mr. Bartlett's life.

The stroke left Mr. Bartlett's speech impaired and his right side paralyzed. In that condition, he was not able to fulfill his teaching commitments, so Gene had to drop out of SMU to take his father's place in schools already scheduled. Once again Gene's formal education had to be put on hold.

The first of these schools was scheduled for Laird Hill, a prosperous oil town in east Texas. Gene was not worried about teaching the music classes, because he was confident about his ability.

But his father had always given an invitation at the close of each school and many people had become born-again Christians as a result. Gene was worried about invitation time. He had never done this. How would he handle it?

He decided to ask a well-known evangelist to speak a few words at the close of the school. The evangelist spoke, but no one came forward. Gene was disheartened.

As always, God's grace proved to be amazing. Gene learned it was God who prompted him to begin singing a new song which had been recently written by his father—as the words of "Victory in Jesus" filled the auditorium, people began to move toward the front to accept Christ as their Savior.

Between each stanza Gene quoted a poem by his father called "Live Your Song." He challenged those attending the school to live a committed life to Jesus Christ, pointing out to them that the lives they lived spoke far more eloquently than the range of voices they had. When the service ended, some fifty or sixty people had made a commitment to Jesus Christ.

Live Your Song
By E. M. Bartlett, Sr.

It's not the words you sing to me,
Or the tune that's set there-to,
It is the life I want to see
And to know the things you do.

It's not the range of voice you have,
To warble high or low,
It's how you live the song you sing
That I would like to know.

It's not the gestures that you make
When to the throng you sing

It is the man behind the song
That I would tribute bring.

For if the man who sings to me
Has failed to live his song,
He fails to touch this heart of mine
Because his heart is wrong.

2

Early Encouragers

Gene still had not decided what area of the music field he would choose, but he leaned toward gospel-quartet music. As he prayed and sought God's direction for his life, there was one request Gene kept asking God to grant—to allow him to be good enough to sing in the great cathedral but also humble enough as a Christian to feel comfortable in the smallest church.

One day, soon after the singing school in Laird Hill, a letter came inviting Gene to come to Batesville, Arkansas, to lead the music for a tent revival to be held in Desha, a small community five miles from Batesville. Reverend O. M. Stallings, pastor of the First Baptist Church of Batesville, was to preach for the two-week revival. Not having anything to do for the next month, Gene accepted. Little did he know at that time that the girl he would meet in Desha—*me*—would become his wife. God was leading in ways that we were not even aware.

The revival was not too successful in decisions for Christ. But from this beginning Desha Baptist Church was organized, and today they have a beautiful modern church building with a good-sized congregation attending.

At the end of the Desha revival, Brother Stallings invited Gene to go to Oil Trough, a nearby community, to help in another two-week revival. He agreed, and for the two revivals he made a total of twenty-five dollars. Not too much money but lots of good experience.

Near the end of the second revival, Gene's parents moved from Dallas to Siloam Springs, Arkansas. His father had left Stamps-Baxter to work for the Vaughn Music Company of Lawrenceburg, Tennessee. Vaughn had no representation in that part of Northwestern Arkansas and Northeastern Oklahoma, so Siloam was chosen as the base of operations. The Bartletts would manage a quartet to do concerts in that area and broadcast from radio station KUOA, located on the campus of John Brown University.

Three pastors had urged Gene to enter the church music field—O. M. Stallings, a boyhood chum of his father who had invited Gene to lead the two revivals that summer; Ford F. Gantt, Gene's pastor when he accepted Christ as his Savior; and James T. Draper Sr., who had been a pastor at Hartford for a short time. This was very encouraging to a young man who was finding difficulty being accepted in Baptist church music circles because of his gospel-quartet background.

Before Gene left Batesville to finish the summer at home in Siloam, Brother Stallings had invited him to be the student director of the First Baptist Church choir and attend Arkansas College, a Presbyterian school located in Batesville. His part-time duties would allow him to participate in college activities. His arrangements for college were unusual in that several members of the church had pledged to pay Gene's tuition, room, and board. Each Saturday morning found the pastor calling on these businessmen and women to pick up their pledges.

Again, God's grace was sufficient, for each week the money was available.

3

Emma-Jeanne's Rain Check

In the fall of 1938 Gene was a second-semester junior at
Arkansas College where I was a sophomore. We renewed
our acquaintance—at least we tried. Gene asked me to attend the first football game of the season as his date. He had
forgotten that he was directing music for an area-wide revival that night. I had to remind him of that commitment.
However, I also asked for a rain check.

Gene became involved in college activities from the beginning. He directed the college pep band which played for the
basketball games, sang in the glee club, and edited the college paper, "The Highlander." He was so busy there was not
much time for dating, but I joined the glee club so that we
might have one activity together.

Sometimes in the afternoons we would go driving in a
Plymouth coupe borrowed from a woman in the church.
Much of our courting was done in that car which we named
"Ole Sal."

My cousin, Gale Bell, and I lived in a private home as companions to an elderly woman in exchange for room and
board. The unheated living room in this home was another
favorite place for dates when time permitted.

At the end of the school year, Gene went home to Siloam
Springs to continue the music business his father could only
direct from his home. Because of his paralysis, Mr. Bartlett
no longer made public appearances.

As do Baptists in many states, Arkansas Baptists met each
summer at their assembly grounds at Siloam Springs for a

time of fellowship and inspiration through teaching, preaching, singing, and recreation. Gene was privileged to attend the assembly that August, walking or hitchhiking the three miles from his home to the campground.

Mrs. J. O. Williams, a chalk artist from Nashville, Tennessee, led an early-morning worship service each day during the assembly. She asked Gene to sing while she gave the message in pictures.

Gene also represented First Baptist Church of Siloam Springs in a talent show. For his number he sang "De Glory Road" by De Wolfe. The preacher for the assembly heard Gene sing and was impressed. He invited him to sing "Stand by Me" at a night service before he preached.

All of this was very encouraging to a young man who had been told that because of his affiliation with the gospel-quartet business he would never succeed in Baptist music circles.

4

Enter B. B. McKinney

In another evidence of God's amazing grace, He planted a man in Gene's life who would make a tremendous impact on him.

The inimitable B. B. McKinney was the song leader for the 1939 Siloam Springs Baptist Assembly when Gene met him for the first time. He was impressed with this giant of a man—his quiet dignity, his ease in directing the congregation and the simplicity of the songs and hymns he selected.

Gene sought a conference with McKinney, and this busy man gave him valuable advice which would influence Gene

throughout his own career. The most important thing B. B.
McKinney imparted to Gene that hot Arkansas summer was
the assurance that if he gave Christ first place in his life,
nothing would be impossible. The encouragement McKinney gave to that shy young man was the turning point in his
(Gene's) career goals. The more Gene prayed the more he
felt God leading him into church music.

The fall of 1939 found Gene enrolled in John Brown University for his final year of college. This was a privately
owned university, taking its name from the founder-owner,
Dr. John E. Brown.

Each student at the university was required to spend a certain number of hours each week working in his or her major
field. Gene worked around the radio station. Among his
several chores was a fifteen-minute solo program which
wasbroadcast weekly.

One of Gene's skills, acquired in the singing schools
where he had studied, was the ability to transpose music.
Part of his work at JBU was to transpose music for guest performers. He also led the student body in a song service before Dr. Brown spoke at daily chapel services.

Gene said that one of his most enriching experiences during those days was hearing Dr. Brown preach and teach the
Bible with clarity and understanding. As he listened to this
Free Methodist preacher, he was able to put into better focus
the leading of the Holy Spirit in his own life.

Money continued to be a scarce commodity in the Bartlett
household. Mr. Bartlett had suffered another stroke. A small
salary from the Vaughn Music Company, whatever the quartet made at concerts, and the sale of songbooks was not
enough to allow Gene to remain in school.

Gene went to the university to withdraw. After all, he
could sing in the quartet and perhaps with him managing
the concerts he would be able to add to their income.

Once again, God proved more than sufficient. Gene was

offered a loan, and arrangements were made for the money to finish the school year. That loan was finally paid off eight years later!

Gene received his Bachelor of Arts degree in the spring of 1940. One of the happiest memories of that occasion was: his father was able to attend graduation and to see his eldest son receive his diploma. Praise God for His grace so amazing!

On August 25, 1940, at 4 PM, Gene Bartlett and I, Emma-Jeanne Stephens, were married in Batesville, Arkansas. Dr. J. R. King, pastor of West Batesville Baptist Church performed the ceremony. A few hours later we left for Siloam Springs. A lack of money and his father's health made a honeymoon impossible, but we did take two days to drive to Siloam.

After the wedding Gene settled into the quartet routine. There were concerts at night in Arkansas, Missouri, and Oklahoma. These concerts were booked close enough to Siloam Springs so they could return each night to do a fifteen-minute broadcast from KUOA at noon the next day.

On weekends the quartet performed in singing conventions in the tri-state area.

It was necessary for us to live with the older Bartletts. We helped to care for his dad as his illness progressed. For the last eighteen months of his life, Mr. Bartlett was confined to bed.

(Top) Reggie Bartlett, Gene and Emma-Jeanne's second son. (Bottom) Gene talked with the children about God and music each week at Falls Creek.

PART III

JOYFULLY SERVE

Grace so amazing,
Grace undeserved,
I'll ever praise Him
and joyfully serve.

Gene felt close to heaven when he was leading a congregation or choir in singing—here he was at Falls Creek.

1

Ohio Street Baptist Church

Gene continued to seek the leadership of God for his life. He had committed his future to Christ and His will and now waited for Him to open the doors.

It was not long before God began to move. Shortly after New Year's Day, 1941, the Ohio Street Baptist Church in Pine Bluff, Arkansas, invited Gene to come and teach a leadership study course with the young people. When the committees learned of Gene's singing convention background, they were skeptical. The church was hesitant about turning the music program over to him.

At the end of the study course, he was asked to stay and try directing the music program for a month. I joined him after a couple of weeks. The church continued to hire him monthly for the next six months.

At this point Gene suggested the church either terminate his services or call him to a permanent position. On June 1, 1941, he was called to his first full-time position as music director.

The church was not very large, running about 250-300 in Sunday School. The salary was not large either—about fifteen dollars per week, but we were able to get by.

Since we did not have a car, we needed to rent an apartment within walking distance of the church. We rented a two-room apartment four blocks from the church for eighteen dollars a month.

The Ohio Street church did not have an educational director (now minister of education) so Gene drifted into this role in addition to his music responsibilities.

The church was a loving congregation. It was the only church we ever served which had more attending what we Baptists called Training Union on Sunday night than Sunday School on Sunday morning. This was true because the church was made up of Cotton Belt Railroad families, and many of the men worked on Sundays. They were free by Training Union time and came to church for the evening activities.

Also, Garland Hunter, the foreman of the railroad round house, was a deacon and also served as Training Union director. He enlisted the men for training and saw that arrangements were made for men who were on call to receive their calls at the church.

Gene says of his experience at Ohio Street, "We were so young and so green in church leadership, but God used us anyway." This only proves that willingness to serve God, plus God's help, can make the difference in everything we do.

Tribute must be paid to a beautiful couple, Ruth and Garland Hunter, who became our parents in the work of the church. They had no children of their own and adopted us. There were many times when they shared a meal with us. It seemed they had an uncanny way of knowing when money and food were getting low. God had always provided for His children, and this friendship begun in the 1940s lasted more than thirty years until Ruth was called home. A couple of years later God called Garland to join her.

The Hunters were the kind of friends who were always there, sharing whatever was needed—a meal, a word of advice, or just listening when there was a problem. Discouragement always turned to determination after a talk with the Hunters and a reminder that God has our times in His hands.

In July, Gene had a two-week revival in Memphis, and I went with him. During the second week, when the mail came, there were three letters. Two were invitations to lead singing for revivals. The third was from the chairman of deacons at Ohio Street Baptist Church. Gene was being "fired" from the church. The letter explained it was not because of his work, but because of a lack of money. This is the only time in his long career that he was terminated. In later years he had much empathy for young ministers of music when they were in similar circumstances. He was able to point out that God was still in control and that He could turn an ugly situation into something beautiful if they sought His leadership.

2

North Little Rock and the Twins

I had become pregnant after our move to Pine Bluff. It was decided that my parents' home at Desha would be headquarters while we tried to put our life together. I would remain there while Gene went for a revival in Jonesboro, Arkansas.

Before that revival came to a close, we had been invited for a one-month revival in North Little Rock, Arkansas. The money Gene would earn in that revival would provide for us for awhile. Surely God would work it out by then.

In North Little Rock, A. D. Muse was the evangelist. As the meeting progressed, the church began to consider Gene to direct their music and education program. They wanted to meet his wife, so I joined him for the fourth week.

He had made some very good friends during the revival, and they made arrangements for us to stay with a family in the church. When it became apparent that we would be moving to First Baptist Church of North Little Rock, I began to look for a doctor there.

The last night of the revival, the church called Gene as minister of music and education to begin immediately. After the services were over, several friends went to the home of J. C. and Ellen Raper for fellowship. These two special people would take us under their wings and become close spiritual advisers.

We retired about midnight. But about two hours later I was rushed to Baptist Hospital where I gave birth to premature twins Frances Maurine weighed three-and-one-half pounds. Larry Eugene weighed four-and-one-half pounds. Twins were indeed a shock to everyone, especially the doctor who was to have seen me for the first time later that day.

That week the *Arkansas Baptist* state paper ran a story that Gene Bartlett had been called to First, North Little Rock, and had already launched "an *enlargement campaign*". Once again, God's loving care had been manifested. The small hospital in Batesville could not have cared for such small babies, and we were fortunate to have the better-equipped facilities of Baptist Hospital in Little Rock.

3

Larry, Frances, and Two Pair of Trousers

After the call to the North Little Rock church and the birth of the twins, the nightmare began!

It was evident I would be dismissed from the hospital, but the twins would have to stay until they were larger and stronger. Gene began to search for an apartment we could afford. The salary at North Little Rock was fifteen dollars per week. When he left there a year and one-half later, he was making twenty dollars per week. The day I was released from the hospital, we moved into a small apartment in walking distance of the church.

The twins would not be allowed to leave the hospital until they reached five pounds in weight. Larry was brought home when he was four weeks old. Frances did not join the family for another three weeks. During that time, since they had to have mother's milk, Gene rode the bus and carried it to them daily.

Once we made it home, we needed help in caring for them. My Aunt Emma came to help out for a few days—she stayed six months!

Because of the small apartment, if one baby cried, it woke up the other. They also had to be fed every three hours, day and night, so Aunt Emma, Gene and I took shifts at night caring for the babies. Gene carried a full load at the church, so he was given the 3-to-7-AM shift. Aunt Emma and I took the first part of the night. It was a busy time.

A little neighbor boy who passed by the apartment each day on his way home from school saw all of the diapers hanging on the clothesline and asked his mother why the Bartletts had so many "pillow cases." (This was before diaper services or disposable diapers.)

Sometime later, just after the bombing of Pearl Harbor in December, 1941, some members of the church had an apartment available in a better area of North Little Rock. It was on the "right" side of the tracks and still in walking distance of the church. So, we moved again.

God blessed the work of the church in North Little Rock, and as it grew Gene learned, by trial and error, what would work and what would not.

There was no time or money for anything except necessities, and Gene's clothes began to wear thin. One day he had to rush home to put on his one remaining pair of trousers when those he was wearing developed a split in the seat.

Occasionally, we would go across the river to Little Rock to window-shop and to get out for awhile on Saturday night. One Saturday, soon after the trouser incident, we were walking along looking at men's suits in the shop windows when Gene laughed aloud. I asked him what was so funny, and he replied, "Oh, I just think it'll be interesting to see how God provides a new suit for me." He didn't have long to wait. The next morning the teacher of a men's Bible class came to Gene and asked him if he would be offended if the class bought him a suit.

Isn't God's grace amazing? This suit had *two pairs of trousers*.

4

Transition at North Little Rock

The people at First Baptist Church, North Little Rock, loved Gene. He was young and willing to innovate.

The pastor had been at the church for many years and had become somewhat set in his ways about how things should be done. The people welcomed fresh ideas from their new music director. The pastor became critical of the work being done and the methods used. Gene had been taught by his father always to support the pastor. His philosophy was to consider the pastor right because he would be right more often than he would be wrong.

With this philosophy, Gene felt after eighteen months that it was time for him to move. Sadly, he did not wait on the Lord but accepted the first position that became available.

One lesson he learned from this experience was: *God has His own timetable and it isn't necessarily the same as ours.* Nevertheless, we moved to First Baptist Church, Blytheville, Arkansas.

It is always a tremendous mistake to run ahead of the Lord. However, God can take any situation and bring glory to Himself. He proved this in our move to Blytheville. God used it for Gene to gain spiritual and professional growth. One privilege Gene had at Blytheville was meeting Gipsy Smith Jr., son of the famous evangelist.

First Baptist Church was an old church, steeped in tradition. The people were sophisticated and wealthy. The church was filled with families who for generations had made their fortunes in cotton and lumber.

World War II was in full swing, and the presence of an Air Force base in Blytheville made housing difficult to obtain. The Lucien Colemans, a lay family in the church, made room in their home for an apartment. Mr. Coleman later was connected with Baptist Men's work. We four Bartletts moved into their home.

It was spring in Blytheville, and the rainy season was on. It rained forty-five days straight, and I shed as many tears as there were raindrops.

After we had been at the church six months, the pastor, Dr. O. J. Chastain, resigned. So, Gene also tendered his resignation to become effective at the same time.

While the move to Blytheville was not in God's divine will, we were sure the move, after only six months, *was* His will. Once more my parents' home was used as headquarters to await God's opening of another door.

5

From Springdale to the Navy

Not long after our move back to Desha, Gene received word from Baytown, Texas, to come in view of a call to the First Baptist Church there. The position carried a tempting salary of thirty-six-hundred dollars per year!

A day or two before Gene was to leave for Baytown, a pastor friend, Ralph Kerley, called and invited him to come before Springdale Baptist Church in Tulsa, Oklahoma, in view of a call as music director. When he found Gene was to be in Baytown the following weekend, Kerley suggested that he come to Tulsa for the Wednesday night service.

Gene agreed to stop by Springdale as a courtesy to his friend, and then he would go on to Texas.

He never made it to Baytown. There was such a sweet spirit in Springdale, and Gene definitely felt God's leading. He called and canceled his visit to Texas.

Some might have thought Gene was mistaken about the church to which God was leading him. The salary at Springdale was much less, but God has never promised He would lead only to positions of more and more money. He *has* promised to guide His servants' footsteps. In that, Gene was quick to testify, "He has never failed me yet."

God's promise to be present has not meant that there were no problems. However, it has meant that while God did not cause the problems, He can use these experiences for strengthening us. The sure knowledge that He knows our needs before we ask, and is only waiting for us to draw close, is very assuring. He wants to bless us in a special way.

The time spent at Springdale was a happy experience. Gene knew that Uncle Sam would be calling him for military duty, so he tried to organize a good music program before that happened.

Perhaps the greatest work he did was with the young people. They were very responsive and the attendance was phenomenal.

After a few weeks in Springdale an unfurnished house became available for rent. One problem—we had no furniture except baby beds and high chairs. Trusting God to provide, we rented the house. It was only about six blocks from the church and was ideal for us since we did not as yet have a car.

The house would be ready for us on Monday. What could we do about furniture? On Saturday Gene's mother called. She was giving up her home in Siloam Springs and wanted to know if we could use any of her furniture.

Isn't God good?

Not long after moving to Tulsa, Gene had a chance to buy a Model-A Ford. It was perfect for visitation. Gas and tire rationing were in effect, but that car did not use much gas, and tires were available. Because of his work, Gene was also issued a "C" ration book for gasoline. People with bigger and better cars were not as fortunate as we were.

I had never learned to drive, but when Gene had a tonsillectomy I was forced to go for medicine. After that, I became braver and would drive the six blocks to church. A policeman often directed traffic on the corner by the church, but not once did he ask to see my driver's license.

As the time drew near for Gene to report to the military, the family moved back to Arkansas. He enlisted in the Navy and was off to see the world.

(Top) Gene received the Doctor of Music degree from Oklahoma Baptist University (left: Dr. William G. Tanner, right: Dr. Warren Angell). (Bottom) Gene conducting the recording session for "Every Day Is a Better Day."

PART IV

LIFE
WORTH
LIVING

Grace so amazing,
and love so divine
Makes life worth living,
and brings joy sublime.

(Top) Gene with one of the joys of his life, The Singing Churchmen of Oklahoma. He's at front right. (Bottom) Recording *Fun Songs for Kids by Paw Paw and Julie* (front left to right: Thurl Ravenscroft, Ralph Carmichael, Julie, and Gene).

1

Navy Boot Camp

In early September 1943 Gene left Batesville for boot camp in San Diego. The twins and I were to stay with my folks for the time being. I taught classes at the high school where I had graduated.

Gene described his trip by train to California as riding in a cattle car. The soldiers were packed in. Gene was put in charge of several recruits, all younger than he, none of whom wanted to be there. Space was limited and sometimes tempers became short. After four or five days they arrived in San Diego to begin ten weeks of rigorous training.

Gene was made "captain of the head" for a period of time. Sound impressive? For you landlubbers, that means he was in charge of seeing that the bathrooms were kept spotless!

Southern Baptist work in California was in its infancy, but Gene hunted up a church which held services in a lodge hall. There he met other young men who shared his interest in helping strengthen Southern Baptist ministry in the state. One of these was George Boston Jr., a young man from Oklahoma who was in the Marines. The two of them helped the pastor with the music and the Sunday School programs. They discovered their parents had been college classmates in Tennessee.

The church rented a hall over a nightclub to hold revival services in downtown San Diego. Gene directed the music for the revival during which his friend George surrendered to the ministry. He is now pastor of First Baptist Church of Cleveland, Oklahoma.

While spiritual decisions were the high point of the revival, a low point was the fact that the building burned during the time the revival was being held. Gene recalled the eerie feeling of seeing everything destroyed except the pulpit stand which the evangelist had used each night.

Gene's bunk mate, whom we'll call Bill, was a young man with such a foul mouth that it was embarrassing to be in the same conversation with him. No amount of asking him to refrain from such language did any good. Bill also made fun of Gene when he read his Bible. So about the only thing Gene could do was pray for Bill and live for Christ before him.

However, God has promised if we are faithful He will bring to pass the desires of our heart. This He did.

When the ten weeks of boot camp ended, everyone was given leave. Gene came to Arkansas. Bill went home also, but he returned earlier than the rest. It was not long before the others learned why. It seemed that Bill had gotten drunk one night and his father had kicked him out. The Navy was the only place Bill had to go.

Soon after the others had returned they were at the service center of First Baptist Church of San Diego after a Sunday night service when Gene saw Bill walk in.

"What in the world are you doing here?" Gene asked Bill. Bill replied that he needed to talk to someone about his salvation. Gene talked with him and asked him to pray. Bill's prayer asking Jesus to come into his heart was interesting but unorthodox.

"_____ _____, Lord, if You're anything like Bartlett says You are, I need You and want You in my life," said Bill. He accepted Christ that night.

It would be wonderful if I could tell you Bill quit cursing immediately. That was not the case, but his language did improve and Gene believed that in time God would cleanse his language as he had already cleansed his soul.

2

Duty in Japan

After the completion of boot camp, Gene was sent to school to become a radio operator. When he knew he would remain at Oceanside for several months, his mother, the twins, and I went to California to be near him.

Housing was impossible to find in the San Diego area, but my cousins, Gale and Paul James, were so gracious to invite us to stay with them until suitable housing could be found.

It was soon apparent that to get housing I would have to work at some type of war-related job. I found employment at Consolidated Aircraft and worked on the assembly line until an office job became available. I was an original "Rosie, the Riveter." After waiting for some time we moved into a three-bedroom apartment in a Federal housing unit. It was close enough that Gene could come home on an overnight pass at least twice each week and most weekends.

As graduation time came closer, it was decided the family would return to Arkansas when Gene was sent overseas. When his day of departure finally came, he was not allowed even to return home to say good-bye.

His first stop was Hawaii and Pearl Harbor. There they waited, getting ready for the invasion of Japan. Fortunately for him the Japanese surrendered before his unit had to go. Gene's group was a part of the Fifth Fleet. He was in what was known as a "beach party," a group that would go in first to set up a communication system.

While Gene did not see any fighting, he did suffer a war-related injury. During maneuvers on the beach, Gene opened a can of K-rations for lunch and cut his hand! They *did not* give a medal for that!

After the Japanese surrendered, Gene spent eleven months aboard ship in Yokosuka harbor in Japan. His was the first ship into the harbor after the bombing of Hiroshima. He had liberty in town only once but reported that the devastation was indescribable.

Gene visited a hospital in Hiroshima that was still in use. On the roof, overlooking miles and miles of destruction, he found a piano. Sitting down, he played and sang "God Is Just a Prayer Away." The doctors, nurses, and patients gathered around and asked for more. Of course, his next song was a stanza of "Victory in Jesus."

Wanting to send me a Christmas gift from Hiroshima, Gene stood in a long line to buy a tablecloth. He did not know until he returned home months later that a label on the cloth read "Made in the USA."

One of Gene's lasting memories from his stay in Japan is of Christmas. The ships around the harbor were shining with Christmas lights as they sent greetings from one ship to another and serenaded with Christmas carols. This was strictly against rules, but, after all, it was Christmas, and they needed the diversion.

3

Mustering Out to Muskogee

When the servicemen had accumulated a certain number of points and could show that a civilian job awaited them, they could get out of the military. Gene began to talk to God about his need for a job.

Soon a letter came from the pastor of White City Baptist Church near Tulsa, offering him a staff position there. It is still puzzling how the letter ever reached Gene. Gene showed the letter to his superior officer and was soon on his way home. Isn't it interesting how God works His wonders?

After docking in Seattle, Washington, Gene was quarantined. Someone on board had typhus fever. It was eventually determined that those who had kept up with their shots could get off the ship, so Gene was released after a week. Thanks be to God that he had had all his shots.

On Sunday morning he attended First Baptist Church of Seattle. There was a large crowd and Gene wound up sitting in the front row of the balcony. A woman downstairs punched her husband and said, "That's Gene Bartlett in the balcony." Her husband didn't think it was Gene, but they decided if he picked up a hymnbook and sang, they would know it was Gene. He did! The young couple were graduates of John Brown University and had known him when he was a student there.

After church the couple invited him to lunch and showed him around Seattle. The next day he was on his way to Batesville. He spent the next few days just enjoying being with his family and getting reacquainted with Larry and Frances. They were so young they had almost forgotten "Daddy."

Soon Albert Lowther, director of missions for the Tulsa Baptist Association, invited Gene to help him in a revival in Sapulpa, Oklahoma. He accepted on the condition that he could bring his family. The church was agreeable, and we were made most welcome at First Baptist Church.

The revival services were wonderful. God was present in mighty outpouring of His saving grace. More than one hundred decisions were made, and most of these were for salvation. You can imagine what an impact that had on Gene. He had been away from good gospel preaching for more than eighteen months and this was a time of spiritual renewal.

At the close of the revival in Sapulpa, we went to look at White City Baptist Church in view of a call. Gene did not feel God's leadership to take the position there.

After our visit to White City, we returned to Arkansas to visit and wait for God to show us what He had planned for our young family. A few weeks later an invitation came from Central Baptist Church in Muskogee, Oklahoma, asking Gene to come for an interview. They were in need of a music and education director.

Gene spent a weekend in Muskogee and after the services on Sunday night the church met in business session and called him. He was so sure of God's leadership that he accepted the call that night.

Within two weeks we were on the field and there began a love affair which is still going on today.

4

Settling In

The pastor of Central Baptist Church was Dr. George Boston Sr., the father of Gene's Marine buddy, George Jr., whom he had met in California.

You may say this was just a coincidence. Gene does not believe God is a God of coincidences, but he does believe God has ordained our paths even before we are born and this was just another instance of His leadership.

The church had many young married couples with small children, and we have some very dear friends among those people. One couple in particular, Ermal and Lewis Windsor, became very close to us. They lived on the next street from the church, but if you went down the alley it was just a short distance. They would leave the key in their car, and when Gene needed one he was free to borrow theirs. Ermal has laughed many times about going out to run an errand and finding the car was gone. She knew, though, that Gene would not be gone too long as he tried not to abuse their generosity.

Gene really liked his work at Central and God blessed the church. Membership was more than 700. On one occasion Sunday School attendance reached 731 during a revival preached by Albert Lowther. Attendance may have been helped by the fact that the pastor had promised to push an orange down the sidewalk with his *nose* if the attendance was over 700. Everyone, including the media, was on hand to see this.

Gene led the choir to do some things they had never attempted before. At Christmas they did the *Messiah* and at Easter, *The Crucifixion*. These were both well received by the church and many from over the city attended these special services. The choir was so happy to have been able to present the gospel message along with such great music as part of their ministry. Gene was equally thrilled to have the opportunity to direct these for the first time.

We experienced at least two other important firsts in Muskogee. We bought our first home (after watching it being built) and we bought a used 1940 Ford. By today's standards neither would be considered elegant, but we thought they were pretty special.

5

Central Experiences

The usual funny and not-so-funny things happened with the twins as they grew.

In the latter category, I remember one Sunday night when we had returned from church and I was hurrying to get the children ready for bed. They were their usual exuberant selves. Frances hopped onto the divan and plopped down pretty hard. She let out a scream, and we discovered she had sat on a crochet hook her Grandmother Bartlett had left in some yarn in the corner of the couch.

We rushed her to the emergency room at the hospital. Can you imagine the strange looks Gene received as he carried his daughter in with a crochet hook dangling from her bottom?

The doctor removed the hook with a very small incision and the next day she was as good as new.

Another time we were having revival services outside on the church property. We always got to church early. One night I was visiting with some older members before services when the twins rushed up. In loud, distinct words they said, "Mama, can we go after church and get some of that 'rotten beer' like we had last night. Please, please!"

You can imagine my embarrassment. I did not even try to explain that they really meant *root beer!*

Still another first for Gene and for the church was taking a group of young people to Falls Creek Baptist Assembly. Little did Gene know that first summer there that God would allow him to become a part of the majesty and wonder of the Falls Creek story.

Central did not have a cabin, but churches were allowed to camp out in tent city. This is what we did for the two weeks of camp. Food never tasted so good. It was a wonderful time. The preaching, teaching, and singing were so inspiring.

Near the end of the second week the ideal weather came to an abrupt end in a downpour of rain. About midnight we were awakened by thunder, and you can imagine our concern for food, clothing, and bedding. Nothing escaped the water. Going barefoot in the mud was not as much fun as when we were kids. However, with the morning light Gene assessed the situation and everyone voted to stay until the end of the camp. Even having to bathe in the creek is not too bad when you are young.

When we returned to Muskogee we had Falls Creek Night, as all Oklahoma Southern Baptist churches do. In the testimonies of our young people the church was made aware of the spiritual impact these two weeks had had on individual lives. One of the most helpful things for the young people who made decisions at Falls Creek was a follow-up ministry where they were instructed and encouraged to put into practice the spiritual truths they had gained.

Gene discovered that it is very easy to fall back into the same old rut once the spiritual "high" experienced at Falls Creek is replaced by day-to-day living and regular routines. Central has never missed a summer sending a group to the assembly. Some years after Gene left Muskogee a cabin was built for their use.

6

Trinity Treat

When Gene had been at Central a year or so, First Baptist Church of Oklahoma City began considering him as music director. However, after praying about the change, he did not feel his work at Central was finished and he declined the invitation.

In July 1947 we were vacationing at my parents' home in Arkansas when Gene received a telephone call from Dr. I. L. Yearby, pastor of Trinity Baptist Church in Oklahoma City. After the telephone conversation we were to visit Trinity the following weekend.

Gene has a letter in his files from Dr. Yearby outlining the things they wanted and expected in the music ministry at Trinity. In the points outlined, Gene discovered the very things he had dreamed of being able to accomplish in a full-time music program—a choir for every age group, plus ensembles, quartets, duets, and great congregational singing. He believes that most people want to participate in worship and that the only audible opportunity for most comes through singing. Gene was impressed with the church and the music committee and we left Oklahoma City with the idea that whatever God's will was in the matter we would be open to His leadership.

The church did call Gene as minister of music and in October, 1947, we moved to Oklahoma City.

Gene felt it was imperative that he begin a program of music that would appeal to all members of the church and this he did. The former music director of Trinity had gone to another church in the city and had taken thirty-two choir members with him.

I would not be telling the truth if I said there were no problems. The first Sunday, there were nine people in the choir and we began to wonder if God had made a mistake. Since we really knew that God is not a God of mistakes, we then thought we had misread His will for us. Surely He would not move us from a place where we were happy, with a good program established, and bring us to one where much work needed to be done. But that is exactly what He did and there began a long association with some of God's choicest people.

Gene would be the first to say that he made many mistakes. Probably the greatest was when he auditioned adult choir members in order to get rid of some undesirable voices. This stirred up a great deal of animosity. He was plagued with telephone calls, always late at night, suggesting, among other things, that he leave town. There were times when he really wanted to leave but God was not ready and Gene knew that without a doubt.

We moved a lot when we first went to Trinity. We lived in houses which were bought by the church as property was made available along Twenty-Fourth Street. These were later torn down and the property used for education and children's buildings and parking.

As soon as we were settled in, the twins began their school career at the old Jefferson Elementary School at Twenty-Third and Western Streets.

Gene began to work toward building a music ministry that would benefit every person who attended Trinity. He realized that not every person would like every anthem, special number, or congregational hymn, but he determined that the music would be varied enough so everyone would find something they liked.

To enable Gene to direct all of the choirs he had a group of choir mothers who helped with the organizational chores. These mothers were enlisted and directed by Virginia Turney. These wonderful helpers seemed to anticipate the choirs' needs and provided for them weekly.

One of the ensembles which gained some fame was known as "The Trinity Trebles." These were ten teenage girls; nine singers and an accompanist. They were invited to sing one summer at the Church Music Leadership Conference at Ridgecrest Baptist Assembly in North Carolina. Of course, they went. They had to pay their own expenses and, to save money, they rode a commercial bus. They had a wonderful time and Mrs. Ella Nichols went along as chaperone. Someone has said that Baptists give more standing ovations than anyone, and this happened each time the girls sang at Ridgecrest. It would be impossible to list the many people who were always ready to help when needed.

Once each quarter Gene presented a Visualized Song Service on Sunday night. These were well received. The slides and music presented were very impressive and the congregation enjoyed singing along. Gene did these before using multimedia in churches became as popular as it is today.

Gene also provided music leadership for every department in Sunday School and Training Union and cooperated with all phases of the work of the church. He provided special music for any department when requested.

About five years after Gene went to Trinity, Dr. Yearby resigned as pastor. The church was without a pastor for seven months. In fact, Gene was the only staff member left during that period. With the help of good leadership in strategic places, the church program continued to go forward.

It became a joke that the minister of education usually left Trinity just before Vacation Bible School and Falls Creek, leaving Gene to carry the load for the staff. Mrs. F. R. Weaver served as VBS principal and together they conducted very successful schools.

During the time the church was without a pastor, Gene was called upon to perform various services which the pastor usually did. One of these was funerals. I questioned him about the legality of this. Since Gene was not *ordained*, I wondered if the person were properly buried.

The pastor search committee recommended Dr. Robert S. Scales, pastor of First Baptist Church of Seminole, Oklahoma, to the church. He became their pastor, beginning a long and loving relationship which still exists. Dr. Scales served for twenty-five years and is now pastor emeritus.

In 1952, our son Reginald Scott was born. We had waited eleven years after the twins. You can imagine my anxiety. They had been premature, and what if I had twins again? My fears proved unfounded and our little son was born April 5, 1952. God knows our needs before we ask and is faithful.

The coming of Dr. Scales to Trinity was not the beginning of the relationship between the Bartlett and Scales families. Inez Scales and Gene had both grown up in Hartford and Dr. Scales was from nearby Greenwood, Arkansas. Even though Gene only remained on the staff at Trinity for two years after Dr. Scales came, it was a time he really enjoyed.

Trinity continued to grow, reaching one thousand in Sunday School attendance. The department for married young people was the first in the Southern Baptist Convention and contributed greatly to the attendance record.

Trinity's music ministry continued to grow from the small beginning on that first Sunday to some three-hundred enrolled in all choirs.

Then God said to Gene, "I have other things for you to do in music ministry in Oklahoma."

(Top) Gene with the 1975 *Baptist Hymnal* containing songs by Gene and his father E. M. (Bottom) E. M. Bartlett's song books were presented to Southwestern Baptist Theological Seminary (left to right) Dr. James McKinney, Gene, and his brother Charles.

PART V

HOW FAR
A LIFE
CAN REACH

Grace so amazing
was bought by God's Son,
Through His deep agony,
vict'ry was won.

(Top) Gene enjoyed narrating *The Old Fashioned Series* and *Shade Tree Musician* while sitting in a rocking chair. (Bottom) Gene was honored with the W. Hines Sims Music Award at the Southern Baptist Convention Music Conference. Dick Ham made the presentation.

1

To State Work and Falls Creek

Late in the summer of 1953, Dr. T. B. Lackey, executive
secretary-treasurer of the Baptist General Convention of
Oklahoma, contacted Gene and asked him to consider coming to work with the convention.

In those days the program of church music was housed in
a department with Baptist student work. Gene would become secretary of that department, directing the student
work on Oklahoma college campuses and helping churches
and church musicians.

In outlining the work Gene would do with Oklahoma
Baptists, Lackey stressed that Falls Creek Assembly would
have an important place in his job.

Falls Creek is located on a two-hundred acre tract of land
in the Arbuckle Mountains south of Davis, Oklahoma. It an-
nually hosts some thirty-five thousand teenagers during a
five-week period in July and August. They come for Bible
study and worship. Evangelism and missions are both important parts of the program. Falls Creek is the largest camp
of its kind in the world.

It had been seven years since B. B. McKinney had directed
the music for the Assembly. Lackey recalled that when
McKinney had led the singing each summer, the young people rode away on the backs of trucks at the close of each
week singing the choruses they had learned during camp.

This was part of the criteria for determining if the assembly had been a success.

After the executive board of the convention met in November, Gene was called as the secretary for music and student work. At the close of the board meeting, one of the committee members asked Gene if he could do the work.

"I don't have any idea," Gene answered, "but I'm willing to try with God's help." He tendered his resignation to Trinity Church on December 7, 1953, to begin his new job on January 1, 1954.

Following are excerpts from Gene's letter of resignation:

> You have been very gracious to me and my family these almost seven years, for which I am very grateful. I also want to thank you for overlooking the many mistakes that I have made through the years. You have made it possible for me to further my training for Christian service and have greatly enriched my spiritual life. Thank you from the bottom of my heart.
>
> Emma-Jeanne, Larry, Frances, Reggie, and I really love Trinity and, with your consent, we would like to continue as members. We have the utmost love and respect for the Robert S. Scales' and the John D. Matthews' [pastor and minister of education and their families] and pledge our complete cooperation to their leadership.

What can we say about Trinity Baptist Church? For forty years it has been our church home. We have some of God's choicest people there and we are privileged to call them "friends." They have loved us in spite of our limitations, and allowed us to love them in return. This loving relationship is still going on today.

Isn't that what church is all about?

2

Music and Student Work

God has promised to equip us for the tasks He calls us to do. Gene leaned heavily on that promise as he began his new job as secretary for music and student work of the Baptist General Convention of Oklahoma.

By Gene's own admission, one of the best secretaries to be found anywhere helped to make his work lighter and more productive. Mary June Tabor came to work in the department as his secretary and remained the entire twenty-six years he served. Her expertise was invaluable to the work. She and I agreed from the beginning that she would have to "keep him straight" at the office while I would undertake the task at home.

Gene has never been a disciplined person. As printing or some other deadline would be drawing near, Mary June would try to get him to make a needed decision. Sometimes he would say, "I'm not ready to make that decision, but keep pushing me." Together, they usually decided in time.

Gene enjoyed working with the college students. His only previous experience with Baptist student work was serving as president of the Baptist Student Union while attending Shenandoah Conservatory in the 1930s. However, he has always liked to be "where the action is" and this gave him that opportunity.

He placed a great deal of emphasis on starting new Baptist Student Unions on every Oklahoma college campus and at the University of Oklahoma School of Medicine, and assisting each group in obtaining a building.

Some of Oklahoma's brightest students could be found participating in BSU activities. Part of Gene's job as state director was to provide strong campus leadership, and in every instance God had someone ready for the job.

While Gene perhaps did not feel adequate for his work with students, he did love them and he listened to them.

He tried to visit each campus often, to attend vespers or noonday devotionals. He led them in sing-a-longs. In sessions like these, he became better able to know the needs of the young people and how to provide for them.

After four years of doing both student and church music work for the convention, the work was divided and Gene became responsible only for music. Dr. Clyde Clayton became director of Baptist student work.

It has been very rewarding for Gene to see men and women in all areas of life manifesting spiritual qualities which began to develop years ago when they were students on Oklahoma college campuses.

Once more, God's grace, so amazing, is evidenced in many of these lives.

3

Equipping Music Leaders

As Gene became able to focus exclusively on the church music programs in Oklahoma Baptist churches, he began to ask God to help him focus on the areas of work most needed.

It seemed that God was leading him to place emphasis on the smaller churches with volunteer or part-time directors. Most of these leaders were dedicated Christians, but many lacked any formal musical training. In searching for ways to implement training in the shortest time, Gene remembered the old-fashioned singing schools where he had learned the fundamentals of music. This could be the answer. For the 1970s, he would call them Fundamentals of Church Music Schools.

In cooperation with the associational leaders, there would be four or five of these going on in the state simultaneously. They were designed for all the churches in the association and met one night per week for nine weeks. Music leaders from all vocations were trained in these sessions. This was a "high-water" mark for training church musicians in Oklahoma.

Gene used local full-time ministers of music as teachers. One teacher had this comment about his participation in one school: "The sounds of do, re, mi, fa are beginning to ring out as the class is taught to a varied and enthusiastic group of pastors, music directors, adult choir members, Sunday School teachers, young people, families, and even some who might be classified as senior citizens. They learn the very basic fundamentals of reading music, singing, directing, and administering a church music program."

These methods worked very well. For example, in Tahlequah, Oklahoma, the school was geared and promoted mainly for the small Indian Baptist churches of the Cherokee (Indian) Association. The superintendent of missions, Reverend J. R. Stogsdill, said: "For most who are enrolled, this is the first opportunity for such a study. It has opened up an understanding of the need for better music programs in our churches and how it becomes an aid in carrying on the work of the Lord. We are realizing a joyful experience."

Gene taught some of the sessions and tried to visit each school at least one night. He provided extra materials to show participants how to make music an integral part of their worship services.

The larger churches which had full-time music ministers did not need such basics. For these directors, Gene had a retreat near the end of each summer. They usually met at a state park for a relaxed time of renewal and inspiration. He used this occasion to bring in well-known and respected choral leaders.

Charles Hirt, professor at the University of California, Los Angeles, was a guest one summer. Others included such top church musicians as Paul Christiansen, Don Hustad, Walter Dahlin, Kurt Kaiser, and Tom Mills.

Ministers of music came from all over the state for two days of listening and learning. Each leader had something unique to offer in organization, interpretation, and presentation. It was a wonderful time of inspiration, and the ministers of music returned to their churches renewed and ready to tackle the new church year with fresh ideas for their choirs.

4

Workshops and Choir Festivals

Continuing his idea that music should involve every member of the church, Gene held music workshops and choir festivals for youth. He continued the annual Youth Choir Festival begun by one of his predecessors, Ira Prosser.

Music directors from churches all over the state brought their youth choirs to the campus of Oklahoma Baptist University in Shawnee for a day of music activity. Choirs were judged for their performances throughout the day and were rehearsed by some well-known and competent musicians for a massed choir evening concert. These festivals were very popular as some twenty-five hundred youth came together to sing praises to God.

Probably one of the most popular events for young people was the Youth Music Workshop. About two hundred youth were chosen by their music directors to participate. They must be outstanding in their local church and their application must be signed by their pastor.

The workshop lasted one week, also on the campus of OBU. The purpose of the workshop was to enrich the lives of Baptist young people through their participation in singing God's praises. Also, the workshop was planned to help participants learn principles of music that would be helpful in any walk of life they chose, assist in developing future church music leaders, and deepen the spiritual lives of the youth through worship experiences.

The workshops became so successful that two separate weeks were held—one for junior-high students and one for senior high. Teachers volunteered to teach, knowing that no salary was involved. The only paid leader was the choral director who led twice-a-day rehearsals and directed the choir in concert on the last night.

Almost weekly Gene receives a letter or two from some young persons telling him how those workshops started them on a career in music. Following is part of one such letter.

It is wonderful to think back on the youth music workshops and even the hot summer days at Falls Creek. I cherish those memories and I'm filled with gratitude to you for making them happen. Your greatest gift to me and many others was to give young kids encouragement and a place to belong in church music. I would not be here today without you and your belief in me.

For the younger children, based on the same format as the youth choir festivals, were the festivals for children's choirs.

These were also held at OBU and gave the children in
Oklahoma Baptist churches a glimpse of the college campus.
Nothing could compare with the enthusiasm manifested by
these youngsters, ages nine-to-twelve years. Gene brought
in the foremost children's choir directors for these events. A
massed choir concert ended the day.

A typical phone call or letter from some of these former
participants goes like this: "Thank you for caring and sharing with a ten-year-old as an individual. Some of your songs
will always be sung. But, more important, some of your boys
and girls in Christ will be singing somewhere around this
world. You touched our lives and we, in turn, will touch lives
who will touch lives until Jesus comes."

I think the one thing Gene wanted to do with these boys
and girls was to "stir up the gift of God" which was in each
of them and to advise them as Paul did Timothy: "Follow the
pattern of the sound words, which you have heard from me,
in the faith and love which are in Christ Jesus" (2 Timothy
1:13, RSV).

5

The Singing Churchmen

Gene earnestly desired to have a group of music directors
from the Baptist churches of Oklahoma come together for a
time of fun and fellowship through singing. In 1961 the first
group met together to rehearse, and the dream of the Singing Churchmen of Oklahoma began to become a reality.

At that first meeting, some thirty men attended. The
meeting took place in Tulsa where the Western Church Music Conference was being held. Their first performance was

at that conference. They were so well received that they decided to keep singing together.

The Singing Churchmen of Oklahoma have grown through the years and only recently more than one hundred men celebrated twenty-five years of making beautiful music.

Gene directed the group a few times, but he wanted the best for the choir and was willing to allow someone else to direct in order that they might achieve the best for Jesus' sake. Dr. James D. Woodward of Oklahoma Baptist University has been the director for many years.

Great and wonderful opportunities have come their way in these twenty-five years.

They have sung at the annual meetings of the Southern Baptist Convention, Oklahoma Baptist State Convention meetings, Oklahoma Evangelism Conferences, the Baptist World Alliance in Tokyo, and Glorieta Baptist Conference Center. They have recorded with Bill Gaither, Ronn Huff, Ralph Carmichael, Broadman, Word, and the Southern Baptist Radio and Television Commission. They have served as the backup group for Robert Hale and Dean Wilder on several of their recordings.

Gene never dreamed when the group first started in the 1960s that they would still be going in the 1980s.

From testimonies of those participating, they may continue until Jesus comes. Some of these young men have been involved in Oklahoma Baptist church music programs since the junior choir festivals. Many have struggled to make a place for themselves in church music.

Gene always told ministers of music in the state he was there anytime they needed him. "If you need something, call collect," he would say. Sometimes they did call collect for a word of encouragement, of advice, or just to talk. These men have been able to draw strength from each other through sharing God's love through music.

As one young man has said, "When I feel like giving up, I

remember the words to a song of yours, Gene, which said, 'Don't you quit and just sit there feeling sorry for yourself; God has better things ahead for you to do.' It is encouragement like this that spurs me on."

The Singing Churchmen of Oklahoma still give concerts about seven months of each year, trying to reach every area of the state. They are always an inspiration to the audience, but the men insist they are the ones receiving the greatest blessing.

As one of the ministers of music has said, "The Singing Churchmen of Oklahoma have given me a place to stretch and grow as a musician. More importantly, I have felt God's presence and the indwelling of the Holy Spirit as we share with each other in song, in testimony and in love. Thank you for your vision so long ago. No other state has such wonderful fellowship as that among the ministers of music of Oklahoma Baptists."

This is just one more example that God is "able to do exceedingly abundantly above all that we ask or think, according to the power that worketh in us" (Eph. 3:20).

PART VI:

HERE IS
MY LIFE

I cannot fathom
why He would love me
Enough to die there
on dark Calvary.

(Top) Gene's last meeting with state denominational music leaders before his retirement. All these men had served in Oklahoma sometime during Gene's tenure: (left to right) Dr. John McGukin, Dr. Charles Sharp, Ervin Keathly, Dr. Bill Reynolds, Harry Taylor, and Bob Woolly. (Bottom) Gene (left) was roasted by friends like Dr. Joe L. Ingram (standing) and Dr. E. W. Westmoreland (right).

1

"This Is Your Uncle Gene"

From Leedey and Pocassett they came—from Tulsa, Atoka, and Muskogee, from Goetebo and Wheatland, from small towns, country crossroads, and big cities, from the very smallest church to the largest. These Oklahoma teenagers and their sponsors arrived at Falls Creek Baptist Assembly near Davis by the thousands.

They came to worship, to draw closer to God, and to reevaluate their lives. They came to listen, to sing, play, and to make new friends. For many, the Falls Creek experience would mean a deeply personal encounter with God there in the Arbuckle Mountains. Their lives would never be the same.

At Falls Creek the benches were hard and the temperature and humidity were high. Sweat ran off faces and dripped onto the ground. Youth who returned for a second or third time checked to see if the initials they had carved on the old wooden benches were still visible. As they took their places under the tabernacle for the evening worship services, there was the sound of a loud hum, not unlike a swarm of bees.

Into this scene stepped a man who spoke into the microphone in a quiet voice, "This is your Uncle Gene. We have come to praise the Lord. Be quiet and participate. Let God speak to you as we worship together."

Four or five thousand teenagers grew quiet. They looked

expectantly toward the platform. Another week of Falls Creek had begun.

In the summer of 1954, the first year Gene directed the music, the Assembly consisted of two one-week sessions. Because of the huge crowds, state convention leaders decided to have three five-day sessions so that they might be able to accommodate the crowds.

Still the attendance grew. Falls Creek was expanded to four weeks and finally to five in 1975, the length it has remained.

For twenty-six years Gene tried through the music to prepare the youth for the best possible response to the Word of God proclaimed each night by many of the greatest preachers in the Southern Baptist Convention. He has always considered his musical tastes middle-of-the-road. He selected these styles of music for Falls Creek during the first few years.

As the 1960s rolled around, the youth of the nation were restlessly seeking answers to questions about life, God, and religion. Their hair was long. Their style of dress left something to be desired, at least from the adult perspective. They were worried about nuclear warfare. They were disillusioned with their world. They blamed the adults for the "mess" in which they found themselves. One thing did not change—they still came to Falls Creek.

In this changed atmosphere, Gene saw an opportunity to try to hang on to these young people for the cause of Christ. He tried to do this through music. In the face of criticism, Gene introduced new sounds among the old hymns. He used some music classified as "gospel rock."

One song that was especially popular with the young people was "O Thou to Whose All-Searching Sight." This was an old hymn text translated by John Wesley arranged in a new setting by a Methodist minister of music, Eugene S. Butler. The words go like this:

O Thou, to whose all-searching sight—
The darkness shineth as the light:
Search, prove my heart, it yearns for Thee:
O burst these bonds and set me free!
O Jesus, Thy timely aid impart,
Raise up my head, and cheer my heart.

The words proclaimed a timeless and glorious message of hope, but the music had a different beat and rhythm. This generation that trusted no one over thirty responded to the message of this song because it was delivered through the style of music with which they readily identified.

2

The B. B. McKinney Chapel

About this same time, the early 1960s, Gene began to use musical instruments in addition to the organ and piano in the worship services at Falls Creek.

Surely God could use the guitar, the drums, and the brass for His glory. Through the orchestra, youth who would never sing in the choir could be involved.

People would drive hundreds of miles to be at Falls Creek the night the choir and orchestra did "The Battle Hymn of the Republic," Handel's "Hallelujah Chorus," "Saved, Saved," or to participate as the congregation sang "The Lord's Prayer."

Music classes were part of the curriculum each week and were taught by volunteers from across the state. As the attendance grew, more classes were offered and places to meet were limited. Also, during class time the choir and orchestra rehearsed. This disturbed the classes and it became appar-

ent that provision must be made for a rehearsal site which
would not disturb other activities.

For several years Gene had dreamed and prayed for a
music chapel, a place which could be used year-round for
smaller group meetings as well as rehearsals during
the summer assembly.

One day Gene felt he had received God's answer to his
prayer. He would have copies of his father's song, "Victory in
Jesus," printed and sell them to raise money for the chapel.
When he told me I didn't say anything, but I thought, *There's
no way under heaven he could ever sell enough copies even to start
the building*.

Gene had the copies printed and I would see our daughter, Fran, and our son, Reggie, sitting in front of the tabernacle before the services, selling the copies for *twenty-five
cents each!* I shook my head in disbelief.

I underestimated God and Gene's determination, as year
after year the copies of "Victory in Jesus" were sold. Of
course, he did not sell enough copies to build the chapel, but
the state convention decided to help with the project. Perhaps this was what God had intended all along.

After the convention was committed to build, things
moved along pretty rapidly. Just as in Nehemiah's day, "the
people had a mind to work" (Neh. 4:6). Once again, God
had manifested His "grace so amazing."

When the chapel was completed, it was named for the
man who had directed music for the Assembly longer than
any person up to that time. The B. B. McKinney Music
Chapel has been a great improvement for choir rehearsals,
counseling sessions, and small-group meetings. It also is
used for conferences throughout the year.

3

Theme Songs and Miniskirts

From the beginning Gene used annual theme songs at Falls Creek. He wanted, through these songs, to encourage the young people, speak to them about their beliefs, and give them a firm foundation upon which to build. Some years he wrote the songs himself to enhance the truths being presented in the study book written especially for that year. These were well received and he still often receives letters from former Falls Creek participants expressing how a particular song met a special need in their lives.

Gene tried to involve the teenagers themselves in the music program. The choir was very popular, and at one time there were eight hundred or more in it. This proved to be too many and Gene established an age limit of fifteen or older. This stabilized the number to about five hundred which was manageable.

One of the interesting things about a Falls Creek choir was that 80 percent of those singing were from small churches of less than 100 members. While Gene directed the congregational singing, he used guest conductors for the choir. These were well-known choral directors who were well received by the young people. Among those who returned many summers were James D. Woodward, William J. Reynolds, Warren Angell, Kurt Kaiser, and Buryl Red.

The piano and organ were played each week by the most talented young people available. This launched some of them into lifetime music careers. Those who came most often were Max Lyall, Richard Huggins, Phil Perkins, Roger

Whitten, and David Danner. Following are excerpts of letters
received from some of these musicians.

How many times I have thanked God for your faithful
goodness to me, your early support of me in seeking
God's plan.

Thank you for a chance to stretch our musicianship.

My greatest joy is the wise counsel you gave me at the
time the Lord clearly called me to Christian service. To a
scared and confused young man, you brought reason and
direction that started me on a path of ministry more than
twenty years ago.

It was your encouragement, guidance, and patience that
led me to become involved in church music. Thank you.

Some people used to ask Gene how he could stand to
spend five weeks every summer in the heat and dust of Falls
Creek. His answer was, "How could I do otherwise? Where
in all of the world could one reach over a quarter of a million
teenagers in that length of time?" During Gene's twenty-six
summers at Falls Creek, more than a quarter of a million
young people participated.

Gene also used as many of the youth for special music as
he could. The soloist and ensembles were auditioned. For
most of the years, he oversaw this task himself. Sometimes
youth would have to audition for several times before he
thought they were ready. He has confessed that, at times, he
was so thrilled when one finally made it, he felt like they
were his own.

One of the things Gene insisted to them was that they
must clear the number to be performed through him. He
would make the final decision as to appropriateness. The
message of every song must be doctrinally sound and glorify
the Lord.

Also, during the days of the miniskirts, he was careful that the clothes of the soloists conformed to the assembly dress code, that skirts must be no more than six inches above the knee. However, when Gene volunteered to do the measuring, no one took him up on the offer!

4

Nearly 100,000 Walk the Aisles

As part of the music-education experience of Falls Creek, Gene wanted the young people to learn about some of the outstanding composers and publishers of gospel music. He felt the best way to do this would be to invite the musicians to Falls Creek as special guests.

Ralph Carmichael came and the teenagers welcomed him as only teenagers can. As they sang his compositions, "The Savior Is Waiting," and "He's Everything to Me" with great spontaneity, Mr. Carmichael, in his immaculate white suit, stood in amazement with tears running down his face.

Ronn Huff, an arranger and publisher, was the special guest one summer. He gave his testimony about his home and family, zeroing in on the importance of youth giving Christ first priority in their lives and stressing that every member needs to work at being part of a family. Many of the young people went home with a new appreciation for their parents. And, yes, some parents saw their children in a new light.

Another guest personality was Bill Gaither. He flew into Gene Autry, Oklahoma, in his own jet, and the young people could not believe he was really there. He could not believe their reception of him. To hear the Falls Creek choir sing the "Praise Medley" of his tunes was especially rewarding

for him. He also was fascinated at the choir's response to the
direction of Dr. Warren M. Angell, a man then in his sixties,
still appealing to the youth through his interpretation and
direction of music, old and new.

These special guests came to Falls Creek at their own ex-
pense. I think they really came to see if the things Gene had
told them about Falls Creek were really true. In every instance they said, "No one can adequately describe Falls
Creek."

On the other hand, the teenagers were so impressed at
meeting the composers of some of their favorite songs. And
the composers were just as impressed to hear five thousand
youth stand and sing their compositions with great feeling.

Perhaps one young person expressed the feeling best
when she called home and said, "You will never believe this!
I'm calling from the cabin of *Gene Bartlett* and I can reach out
and touch *Bill Gaither* while I eat homemade ice cream."

While the worship services usually went very smoothly,
there were times when problems arose. Gene demanded
great discipline from the accompanists. If one got ahead or
behind Gene's directing, he has been known to walk over
and direct the individual while standing in front of them. To
keep that many people, singers, and instrumentalists, together, he had to have total commitment and concentration.
Gene could be a hard taskmaster, but the accompanists
knew he loved them and respected their talent. That is why
he used only top performers each summer.

While disturbances were few during the worship services,
one summer during the choir number a disturbed woman
climbed the director's platform and began shouting. The director kept the choir singing while the ushers led the woman
away.

Far more important and memorable than the occasional
problems which arose was the invitation time each evening.

As the strains of "I Have Decided to Follow Jesus" could be

heard, hundreds of young people went forward in response. They came for salvation, for rededication, for special service, and for forgiveness. They came with friends and they came alone.

Many who came would never be the same after the Falls Creek experience. Today, around the world, these young people, now adults, are serving Jesus Christ.

In the twenty-six years Gene directed the invitation hymns, a total of 96,768 young people walked the aisles and surrendered their lives to His service. Is it any wonder that Gene loved Falls Creek and was willing to spend his summers helping Oklahoma teenagers find God's will for their lives?

Yes, God's "Grace So Amazing" is the Gene Bartlett story.

5

Kiamichi Memories

During his tenure in the Oklahoma Church Music Department, Gene was invited occasionally to the Kiamichi Baptist Assembly in the Kiamichi Mountains of Eastern Oklahoma. It was a much smaller camp than Falls Creek, but Gene enjoyed being there and was able to touch lives for Christ and church music, as the following excerpts from letters he received recently will show.

What memories of Gene Bartlett are flashing through my mind today. The first time we met at Kiamichi, he looked like a movie star to me. Then the thrill of being invited, years later, to direct the choir at Falls Creek on three different occasions. Precious memories, how they linger.

A blessing for me through your ministry was an evening at Kiamichi Baptist Assembly, only two months after I had prayed to receive Christ. You were our special guest for the evening and led us in a time of congregational singing that remains a highlight of my life. It was only a part of one evening in a young man's life, but as I look back on it, I believe there has been an abiding difference in my life because God was able to work through you in that service.

Praise God from whom all blessings flow. Sometimes we never know when we have helped someone, but Gene has been blessed in great measure because so many have written to express appreciation for his warmth, his understanding, and his prayerful concern for those young Oklahoma ministers of music whom he proudly called "his boys."

6

Summer Song Harvest

Gene often said that you never know when you've written a song how good it will be until someone sings it. This proved true with the annual theme songs he wrote and used at Falls Creek.

In one of his first years at Falls Creek, Gene wanted to honor the memory of his father, so he used "Victory in Jesus." This great gospel song has become a favorite of many denominations, in addition to Southern Baptists. The summer he used "Victory in Jesus" for a theme song was also when he began selling copies of the hymn to build the music chapel.

Mr. Bartlett wrote "Victory in Jesus" late in his life after he had suffered a stroke and was partially paralyzed. As his earthly body grew weaker, he began to think of heaven and his resurrected body. There would be no more sickness—"I heard about his healing." He thought about the beauty of heaven—"And I heard about the streets of gold beyond the crystal sea." He looked forward to being released from his pain—"And some sweet day I'll sing up there the song of victory."

This was the last song that Mr. Bartlett wrote before he died in 1941. Gene called it a fitting postlude to a great Christian life.

In 1963, Gene used as a theme song "You're Not Alone," his first gospel song published by Broadman. He wrote it one Sunday morning as he sang with the Trinity Baptist Church choir. A visiting preacher was in the pulpit that morning and his sermon was on Job. As Gene looked out at the congregation, many of whom we had laughed and cried with for many years, he wanted to assure them, "You're not alone, God knows your needs, And will supply them. Have faith in him; Just trust the Savior . . . God's grace will see you through."

Many of his friends had lost loved ones and many had burdens almost too heavy to bear, but through these words, Gene could remind them that God was always there and they would never be alone when they let Him have full control. This message was just as meaningful to the youth at Falls Creek.

As the 1960s wound down, Gene noticed that youth who came to Falls Creek were once again more polite, their hair and dress more neatly groomed, they were not as restless, and they responded in a more positive manner to the messages, both in word and music.

Gene always walked to the tabernacle early to prepare for the evening worship. Most of the campers were in their cabins having the evening meal and he liked to use the quietness of the hour to talk to God and to let God speak to him.

On one such evening, he felt God's presence so strongly that as he crossed the baseball diamond, he looked up and said aloud, "God, You did it! The young people have passed through their rebellious years, and I thank You for allowing me to be a part of it. Thank You for not giving up on them or allowing Oklahoma Baptists to give up."

7

Mission '70: Here Is My Life

In the late 1960s, leaders of the agencies of the Southern Baptist Convention were planning a national missions meeting for college students in Atlanta, Georgia. It was to be called Mission '70 and would be held at the end of December 1969, climaxing on New Year's Eve with a worship service ushering in the decade of the 1970s.

Gene was on the program committee and he and Ed Seabough, then of the Home Mission Board, were asked to write the theme song for the meeting. They wanted the song to be a commitment to Christ and to reflect the times in which these students found themselves. Ed wrote the words to "Here Is My Life" and Gene wrote the music. He has often said he thinks the words to this song are perhaps the greatest written for the twentieth century.

More than five thousand college students came to Atlanta that last week of December. They were able to meet Convention leaders, explore hard questions, become involved in mission action projects, worship, sing, and make lifetime commitments.

Gene said one of the great thrills of his life came as the students stood and sang the theme song. As the old year of

1969 gave way to the new year of 1970, all five thousand voices were raised in singing, "I cannot wait, I cannot wait! . . . Here is my life, I want to give it serving my fellow-man, doing the will of God."

Dr. Claude Rhea stepped to the microphone and told the young people that the man who wrote the music was present. He then called Gene to the platform to lead them in singing.

As the new year and the new decade were born, the students sang "Here Is My Life." When they had sung it through, they didn't want to leave and yelled, "Sing it again." So, accompanied by the Atlanta Symphony Orchestra, they sang the first stanza. Then Gene held up two fingers, telling them to sing the second stanza. The students went wild. Gene didn't know what was happening. When Gene had raised two fingers, the students thought he was giving them the peace sign so popular at that time. They thought he spoke their language and they took him in in a warm and special way.

For Gene, the moment was again a time of absolute surrender of his own life to God's grace so amazing.

8

Falls Creek Songs

One day, while driving to the office, Gene was listening on the car radio to a religious station. As the announcer signed off he said, "Well, folks, I have to leave you. Have a good day. But remember, every day will be a better day if you give it to the Lord."

Gene pulled over to the curb and wrote the statement

down on the back of a bank statement. Some weeks later he was in the home of Jack and Beverly Terrell in Dallas. He and Beverly wrote the song, "Every Day Is a Better Day—When You Give It to the Lord." This was a very popular Falls Creek theme. The young people seemed to like the chorus, especially as they were challenged to "hear His call to surrender all—and to live abundantly. Every day is a better day when you give it to the Lord."

One year in the mid-1960s Gene had written "I Believe" as a theme song. The teenagers sang it at Falls Creek, but he knew they were not listening to the words. They sang it simply because it was the theme song. Gene had written it after reading a book by Dr. Lavonn Brown, pastor of First Baptist Church of Norman, Oklahoma. Gene had tried to say in the song things he wanted the youth to know about Christ, the Holy Spirit, and the Bible. He emphasized the reliability of God and the constancy of the church.

God led him to use "I Believe" as the theme song a second year, something he did only that one time. That God was leading was evidenced by the way in which the youth accepted the song that year and by their comments. The phrases "I believe He's equal for this hour" and "I can count on Him" became very real to them as they discovered "His church is here to stay."

In trying to strengthen young people in their beliefs and to help them in their daily walk with Christ, Gene and Betty Jean Chatham wrote and used as a theme song, "Christ Lives in Me." He hoped to inspire them to share Christ with their friends and to rely on His love in every situation.

"God's Grace Is Enough for Me" was written by Gene and used as a Falls Creek theme song just one year before we learned Gene had Parkinson's Disease. We know God gave him this song for his own encouragement. "God has never promised a day without tears; He has never promised a day without fears; He gives grace for today in His own gracious way; His grace is enough for me," Gene wrote in a song that has ministered to many as it does to us. When things get rough, we read the words often—"He will never leave us, nor ever forsake us, He will give assurance—whatever comes our way." I would not have you believe that we never question, never wonder why, but always, "He gives grace for the day in His own gracious way, His grace is enough for me."

It was traumatic for Gene as he neared the time when he knew he could no longer lead the music for Falls Creek. As the Parkinson's put a greater drain on his energy, he wanted one last theme song to help him as well as the hurting, lonely, disillusioned, ready-to-give-up person in the pew.

One night in December, 1978, we were at a Christmas party. Mrs. Tabor, mother of Mary June, and a dear friend of ours, was having health problems also. Gene made a pact with her—if she would not give up he would not give up. Later the song, "Don't You Quit," was born and dedicated to Mrs. Tabor.

This song was the theme song for 1979, the last year Gene directed the music. The young people seemed to sense it was a farewell to an era that had spanned twenty-six years and they sang with a special fervor.

One stanza says, "Do you ever reach the place you want to quit and chuck it all, and you feel that you are fighting all alone? Then try the plan God has made especially for you. It will help you to regroup and carry on." This became a favorite for Gene as he began a new phase and a new plan for his life. In the refrain it says, "Don't you quit and just sit there feeling sorry for yourself—do your bit in helping others find God's plan"—Gene always tried to help others as they called or came by for his counsel. As one young minister of music wrote, "I have tried many times to analyze what it is that you have done that God should use you so mightily. I have come to the conclusion that it is your availability both to God and to us."

During the last week of Falls Creek in August, 1979, Gene knew the time had come for him to resign as director of music for Oklahoma Baptists. It was a sad time as on the last day he stood to one side of the tabernacle with Dr. Joe Ingram, executive secretary-treasurer of the Baptist General of Oklahoma and told him he could not carry on any longer. He could no longer give his best.

As Gene looked out over the sea of teenagers, as he had done so many times before, he prayed that the decisions made for Christ would make a difference in the lives of Oklahoma Baptists and Southern Baptists throughout the nation and the world. He thanked God for allowing him to be a part of this assembly for so many years. He felt privileged, but he also felt humbled that he had been chosen for the task.

In November, the Baptist state convention was to meet in Tulsa and Gene would formally resign there. He wanted me to participate in his resignation speech. If I saw him becoming too emotional I was to lighten things up with a funny story. He told his fellow workers just how much they meant to him and how his life had been enriched by their belief and trust in his work.

I thought it very significant that our first work in Oklahoma churches was in Tulsa and more than thirty years later his resignation also took place there.

From the very beginning of his surrender to God in the field of church music, Gene tried to be open to His leadership. He also kept the door to his office open to those who came by.

Some years after his retirement, Grace Hawthorne, a lyricist from Atlanta, Georgia, and co-composer of the musical, *Shade Tree Musician*, wrote these words about Gene: "What we did, we liked. We used our talents faithfully—surely the Lord is pleased with me."

I think the Lord *is* pleased with Gene and his years at Falls Creek.

PART VII

OUR LIVES
ARE SONGS

Our lives are songs. God writes the words,
    And we set them to music at pleasure;
And the song grows glad, or sweet, or sad
    As we choose to fashion the measure.
                                    —Anonymous

(Top) The Gene Bartlett family and the Charles Bartlett family in a reunion. (Bottom) Governor George Nigh declared "Gene Bartlett Day" throughout Oklahoma. (Note: All pictures herein were gathered by Emma-Jeanne Bartlett with the help of family and friends.)

1

Church Music—Forerunner of the Word

As the years passed, Gene formed ideas and philosophies concerning music and its place in worship. Some of these he discarded, some he refined, and some remained the same throughout his career.

In putting together this chapter, I drew from many articles Gene wrote for the church newsletter while he was minister of music at Trinity Baptist Church. Others I drew from interviews, printed and taped, along with rap sessions with Gene.

Gene believed that music in the worship service, when well planned and rightly sung, is the forerunner announcing the gospel to be proclaimed by God's minister. Every person present must have the opportunity to take part in this great and happy worship of the Lord. Certainly, there must be good special music by a soloist, ensemble, or choir, but there must be congregational singing, as well. Gene provided both.

He also believed that even to be a good listener to Christian music, one must be trained. So while he was minister of music at Trinity, one year he brought one of America's greatest song leaders, Homer Rodeheaver, and a staff of workers to lead a music week for every member of the church.

Gene also stressed that the music department is not the *show* or *performance* department of the church. Musicians are to be creators of spiritual atmosphere. If they fail to achieve this purpose, they miss the mark altogether. Succeeding at the goal requires right attitudes and awareness that music provides clear channels through which personal worship takes place.

In each church Gene served, he tried to put himself and the choirs in the background, allowing God to speak to each listener through the music. I am sure the choir members at times got tired of his constantly reminding them to be cognizant of the words of the hymns and anthems they sang.

"Loud singing is not always inspiring," Gene emphasized. He found that a congregation usually gives a piece of music the right dynamics when they are sincerely moved by the message of the composition. And "mechanical gyrations" by the conductor do not necessarily indicate he is providing the best interpretation of the song.

As minister of music, Gene urged choir members not to see the choir as an entity in itself or to only be interested in the music ministry of the church. Rather, he emphasized the work of the entire church and sought to make the music department an integral part.

Gene believed the "people in the pew" must be the focus of a church's music ministry. The message of hymns and anthems must speak to people in a personal way—to the pain of broken relationships, to loneliness and discouragement. Music must be based on Bible teachings which communicate truths about God and his loving-kindness.

In selecting music, Gene declared that the great anthems are certainly worthy to be sung. At the same time, he maintained that since most Southern Baptists attend small churches or come from small churches, that hymns and gospel songs may more readily speak to their personal needs.

Gene liked the current trend toward including choruses in worship services. Many of these are tunes set to Scripture and are simple enough to be sung by children, allowing them to actively participate in "big church."

Gene insisted for years that a person's love for music must be nourished from early childhood. Once, we received a letter which supports this idea from Tim Jenkins, who grew up in Trinity church when Gene was minister of music. Tim is now a tenor with the New York Metropolitan Opera. He wrote:

> As a young child at Trinity, I first heard your music and was extremely moved. I remember particularly one service when you sang a solo. My parents said, "That's the man who writes the music." The spirit in which you sang was so extraordinary that I determined that somehow I, too, would be involved in music.
>
> I was no more than seven or eight at the time, but I started reading books about great composers. And I started to "compose" so I could be like you. My patient mother would sit at my side at the piano and transcribe what I "composed." I felt on my way.
>
> I have had the opportunity to work with the greatest musicians in the world, but it was you who God used to give me the knowledge and vision of ministering His word through music.

God's people are by nature a happy people and Gene challenged the music leadership to help in creating an atmosphere of joy and a desire to worship through music.

He believed that a portion of every choir rehearsal should be spent in simply reading and absorbing the words of the hymns and anthems. Only then will the music be as meaningful as it can be as musicians give songs the proper interpretation.

Gene also emphasized the importance of the accompanist in helping to lead people in the congregation to want to sing. Addressing this need was only one of the reasons why Gene, as state music director, sought to see that the leadership in every church had learning opportunities.

For those in the congregation who did not sing, Gene invited participation by asking them to open the hymnal and read the words of the hymns as they were sung. Through the years, he had many people tell him that they had never done this before and, after reading the words, the message of a particular hymn meant much more to them.

Most of all, Gene admonished music leaders to make sure the music they use and listen to is pleasing to God and that it would draw people to Him. He quoted Paul in his Letter to the Corinthians as he urged the people to "sing with the spirit, and sing with the understanding" (1 Cor. 14:15).

2

"Sing with Grace in Your Hearts to the Lord"

When Gene reached the age of forty he suddenly realized that a major part of his life was over, never to be recalled. If he planned to write music, Gene realized he needed to get started. He felt that through songs, cantatas, and musicals he would be able to give to his fellow believers a legacy that would last.

Gene approached music composition with the spirit of Paul in Colossians 3:16:

Let the Word of Christ dwell in you richly in all wisdom, teaching and admonishing one another in psalms and hymns and spiritual songs, singing with grace in your hearts to the Lord.

Composing music was not in Gene's job description, so he became a weekend composer. Sometimes when he was in revival in another city, he would take along a portable pump organ to use in working on his songs. Gene was not an instrumentalist and used to tell me he played for his own amusement and sometimes to his amazement.

The portable pump organ was a special one lent to him by his friend, Dr. William J. Reynolds, formerly director of the Church Music Department at the Southern Baptist Sunday School Board and now a professor of church music at Southwestern Baptist Theological Seminary. The organ had belonged to Bill's parents, Mr. and Mrs. George Reynolds, and had been used at Falls Creek Assembly in the early 1920s and 1930s.

As Gene gave thought to the content of a hymn, a gospel song or anthem, he had the conviction that the greatest text to be set to music would be the holy Scriptures. Next would come songs based on biblical truths, but not directly quoted from the Scriptures. Last would be songs written in everyday language to help people express their devotion to God and lead them to walk worthy of His calling.

I believe Gene was able to accomplish the purpose of proclaiming the gospel through every song he has written. They speak of God's love and grace, of His willingness to share His love in day-to-day living.

Years ago a pastor commented, "The thing I like best about the songs Gene Bartlett writes is that not many words are sung before God, Christ, and the Holy Spirit are mentioned."

One day at Trinity Baptist Church two young sopranos came to Gene and asked him to write a duet for them to sing at a revival which was coming soon. One of the women, Gayle, added this request, "Don't let Mary's part go any higher than mine."

Gene could never resist a request like that. "All the Way My Saviour Leads Me," a new setting to a familiar hymn text for two equal voices was the result.

After hearing the song, one young man wrote: "The first

time I heard your setting of the Fanny J. Crosby text I was overwhelmed by the beauty and expression of this work and knew then that it was from God."

A colleague, in writing about the composition, said, "Many of your songs have been sung with great joy by countless numbers of people across the United States and other lands. I remember a special feeling of joy in February 1979 in Seoul, Korea, when I heard a Korean choir singing in their language your setting of 'All the Way My Saviour Leads Me.'"

When the Southern Baptist Church Music Conference was planning their 1977 meeting in Kansas City, they commissioned Gene to write a song to be used at the conference. He turned to the Bible as he began to search for God's leadership. As he read of the great faith of Moses, Job, and David, he determined that he wanted to write about that faith. But he also wanted to show that these were ordinary men whose faith in God made the difference.

"It Takes Faith" was a tribute to these men of old, but it also pointed to the faith that a person needs just to get through the day. I think one of the greatest truths expressed is in the line, "for God remembers where you are and what you do; it takes faith that he will guide you and will help you see it through." Then there is the evangelistic message in the song for those who need to know Christ as their Saviour, "It takes faith in Christ the Savior to save souls like you and me."

For many years the Thanksgiving eve service at Trinity was a service of testimony and praise. On one such occasion Gene noticed that almost everyone who spoke mentioned how God's love had been manifested in their lives. As they spoke of heartaches, tragedies, temptations, and disappointments that had come during the year, one phrase kept recurring—God's love had sustained them through every trial.

In the next few weeks as he reflected on these testimonies, Gene wrote "God's Love Sustains Me." As the words say, "Though storms of life come to threaten each day, billows of sorrow may sweep o'er my soul, God's love sustains me each step of the way." In every instance these faithful men and women of the church were taking God at His Word and could say with the psalmist David, "The Lord is my rock, my fortress, my shield, in Him will I trust."

A song that meant so very much to Gene is "He Will Send the Blessing If You Pray." About six years after her husband passed away, Mrs. Bartlett was cleaning out an old trunk and found those words written by Gene's father. He thought they were worthy of being set to music. Through the years we have had many occasions to need the Savior's power and have found He does indeed have blessings to spare when we go to Him in prayer. He *will* surely send the blessing if we pray.

Gene sometimes told preachers that he wrote during their sermons, and added facetiously that it helped him stay awake. The idea for "He Cared and Took Me In" was born during a message by Dr. Grady Cothen, president emeritus of the Southern Baptist Sunday School Board in Nashville, Tennessee. In his sermon Dr. Cothen talked about how hard it is to care for all the people who need help. He added, "I am so happy that God cares for everyone, for He cared and took *me* in."

Gene jotted down the phrase, "He cared and took me in," and later finished the lyrics and music. The song speaks of God's unconditional love, the love that reaches out to sinners and admonishes us to reach out to others also. The last phrase says, "Thank God, You took me in. Thank God, You took me in."

In addition to using choruses by others in worship, Gene wrote some that he called folk tunes. One popular one is "God Has Something to Say." He pointed out that the noise and clamor all about us make it difficult to hear God speak. He posed the questions, "How can you know that He cares? How can you hear the right voice?" He then provided the answer, "Listen, listen, pay close attention! God has something to say."

Using the language of the 1960s to capture the attention of youth, Gene wrote "What Do You Talk About?" He called on the Christian young person to "wake-up, talk-up, Jesus Christ gave His all! Trust Him, get smart, do His will, hear His call. What do you talk about, Christian?" He then used Fanny Crosby's familiar words to challenge Christians: "Tell me the story of Jesus, write on my heart every word. Tell me the story most precious, sweetest that ever was heard."

Early one Monday morning, Gene met his co-worker, Laddie Adams, director of the Brotherhood Department for Oklahoma Baptists, in the parking lot at the Baptist Building. As they greeted each other, Gene asked about his family. Laddie replied that they had just learned their beautiful teenage daughter had diabetes. As they talked about the disease and how it would affect Jana, Laddie shared a conversation they had had soon after returning from the doctor. Jana was asking her mother about certain favorite foods and if she would be able to eat them. As the conversation progressed, Jana suddenly realized her mother's pain and said, "Don't worry. Everything is gonna turn out all right. Just you wait and see."

Gene went on to his office and wrote down Jana's statement. Soon he wrote the words to "Everything Is Gonna Turn Out all Right, Just You Wait and See." One night Gene and I took the song to the Adams' home to let Jana and her parents hear what he had done with her statement of faith. An accomplished pianist, Jana played for Gene to sing the song. She is now married and her words about herself have proven true. Everything *has* turned out all right.

Gene had a friend, Dr. Sam W. Scantlan, for many years

the manager of Falls Creek Baptist Assembly, who wrote several sets of lyrics which he then set to music. One of these, "The Star of Jacob," Gene later made part of a Christmas cantata. The song was originally written as the theme song for a live Christmas drama staged by the Baptist Boys Ranch Town in Edmond, Oklahoma. Later, several ministers of music in the area asked Gene to write a Christmas cantata, requesting only that he "write us Christmas according to Bartlett." "From the Star to the Cross" traces the life of Christ from His birth to His death and resurrection. It is written so that a smaller church can perform it as well as larger churches.

Gene's efforts on this cantata and other music drew the comment of a colleague who said, "I'll never forget your concern for the small church and, at the same time, your desire to inspire us to heights of musical excellence."

Perhaps one of Gene's better-known hymns is "Set My Soul Afire." The lyrics came one Sunday as he sat listening to Robert Scales preach on "The Thirst that Cannot Be Quenched." He later set the text to music. It is included in the 1975 edition of the *Baptist Hymnal* and has been translated into Spanish and Portuguese. Also, Oklahoma Baptists have used it several times as the theme song for simultaneous revivals.

During one of these revivals, a group of ministers of music appeared on a local television station and sang, among several songs, "Set My Soul Afire." Later in the coffee shop at the hotel where they were staying, the men were recognized by a waitress who said, "Oh, I just saw you on television and I really liked the song you sang." When asked what song, she replied, "It was something about 'getting hot for God.'" You can imagine the ribbing Gene took over that!

On a more serious note, in 1969 a letter came to the editor of the Oklahoma *Baptist Messenger* from a missionary in Sao Paulo, Brazil. The missionary, a former Oklahoma pastor,

Richard B. Douglass, wrote about Gene and Bill Ichter, music secretary for the Baptists of Brazil. He wrote:

> During the recent South Brazil Mission meeting, we almost felt we were back in Oklahoma. The theme of the meeting was "Set My Soul Afire." We opened every session with Gene Bartlett's song by that name. I got the strongest emotional tug when Bill Ichter was leading it. I remember, just before leaving the States, seeing Gene leading "Christ the Only Hope" which Bill wrote. Great gospel music has a way of ignoring boundaries of race and country and blessing people everywhere. It expresses so well our common bond in Christ. The Brazilians are as receptive when my wife sings Gene's song in Portuguese as Americans were to Bill's music. . . . It is a joy to work wherever the Lord leads.

A tragic footnote to this letter is that Richard and Marilyn Douglass later returned to Oklahoma where he was pastor of Putnam City Baptist Church in Oklahoma City. They were murdered in their country home by two transients.

In 1968, Gene was commissioned by Dr. Claude Rhea and the Foreign Mission Board to write a song to be used for foreign-missions night at the Southern Baptist Convention that year. Gene likes to tell that he began the lyrics while sitting in a boring meeting in Nashville. "Tell the Good News" came from that beginning. Someone has said that if songs like this are the result, Gene should attend more boring meetings.

"Tell the Good News" was premiered as missionaries from around the world carried the flags of their nations and wore the native dress of those countries. Southern Baptists were challenged to enlarge their part in telling the good news throughout the world. The vast audience took up the refrain, "Tell the good news that Christ has come; Tell the good news, tell the good news, Tell the Good News to ev'ryone."

As they sang, the auditorium was encircled by missionaries. Gene and I could not help but think of the words of 1 Chronicles 16:23: "Sing to the Lord, all the earth; Proclaim the good tidings of His salvation from day to day"(NASB).

3

Golden Gospel Echoes

For several years Gene had wanted to arrange some of the songs which he remembered from his gospel quartet days and the singing conventions. He had hesitated because he did not want to embarrass his denomination or his colleagues with songs which some had defined as a "lower class of gospel music."

In earlier years, some pastors had objected to the singing conventions on the grounds that they lured people away from church attendance. While this may have been true in some areas, many rural churches only had preaching one Sunday each month. The other Sundays were spent in gospel singing.

As preparations began for the celebration of our nation's two-hundredth birthday, the entire country took a look backward. As Gene reflected on his own beginnings, he wanted to pay tribute to his heritage. Arranging some of his father's songs would be one way to do that.

While some composers write primarily for choirs and other musicians, Gene turned his attention to people he believed were too often overlooked—the people who sit in the pew week after week. It was this approach that probably explains the public's acceptance of the nostalgic *Old-Fashioned Series*.

The first in the series was "The Old-Fashioned Meeting" and is a presentation of music in the style used by Homer Rodeheaver in the Billy Sunday revivals.

It has such old songs as "A New Name in Glory," "His Eye Is on the Sparrow," and the title song, "The Old-Fashioned Meeting." These songs express so well the revival meetings of the 1920s when old-fashioned people, filled with old-fashioned grace, met and prayed for sinners. God heard and souls were saved.

The collection was premiered at our church in Oklahoma City. It was performed on a Sunday evening on the parking lot with everyone dressed in old-fashioned clothes. From this beginning, other churches in several states began to have similar performances. The churches were free to make their productions as simple or as elaborate as they chose. Some included dinner on the ground, bean suppers, antique shows, antique car rides and sometimes even rides in horse-drawn buggies.

The success of these productions found Gene traveling into several states to serve as narrator. Sometimes he wore overalls and sat in a rocking chair as the choir performed. Some of his friends kidded him about creating this just so he could sit and rock. It was very rewarding to see the glow of happiness on the faces of the people—the older generation especially—as they heard a favorite song once again.

While Gene paid tribute to his heritage of gospel music through the first collection, it did not include any of his father's songs.

A second collection, "The Old-Fashioned Singing," was published in 1976 and included arrangements of "Everybody Will Be Happy Over There," "This World Is Not My Home," "We Shall Rise," "I'll Fly Away," "I'll Meet You in the Morning" and "Victory in Jesus." The album has a kind of bluegrass background with guitar, harmonica, and banjo. The title song is the only song written by Gene.

I suppose he had a favorite in each collection and, in this one, "The Old Account" is his favorite due to an experience he had when he was working on the arrangement in his studio on the east side of our home. Gene recalled sitting at the piano near the window early one morning, working on the arrangement, when he felt God's presence very strongly. As the sun streamed through the windows he almost expected to look up and see Christ standing there. He had a very real worship experience as he thanked God that his "old account" had been settled many years ago when he was an eleven-year-old boy.

The third collection in the series is "All Day Singin' with Dinner on the Ground." Gene wanted to use some of the lesser-known tunes of his father and also capture the spirit of the gatherings of Christians for gospel singing and eating the noon meal together.

This collection has arrangements of titles such as "Farther Along," "I'm Not Ashamed," "The Pearly White City," "How Beautiful Heaven Must Be" and "Just a Little While." Our grandson, Scott, was listening to the tape one day and asked, "Paw Paw, why did they sing about heaven so much?"

Gene told him that these were songs out of the Depression days and times were so hard that perhaps people thought a lot about heaven and a land of plenty. This explanation seemed to satisfy Scott and maybe that *did* explain what he called "heaven songs."

One of Mr. Bartlett's songs in this collection, "I Heard My Mother Call My Name in Prayer," was written after he came home late one night and heard his mother pleading with God to save her boy.

The last collection in the series, "The Brush Arbor Meeting," was published in 1981, a year after Gene's retirement.

Among Gene's earliest recollections were people gathering at a brush arbor for evangelistic services. He recalled that several communities would often join forces for a revival. They would choose an area accessible to all, perhaps at a county crossroad, and build a brush arbor for a meeting place. The arbor consisted of poles with boards laid across the top and tree branches over the boards to make a cover. Thus, it became a *brush* arbor. Sawdust was spread on the ground to help control the dust.

People traveled to what they called a "protracted meeting" in buggies, wagons, Model-T Fords, on horses, mules, or walking. In spite of the weather, wind, and dust, thousands were won to Christ during brush arbor meetings which began as early as 1900 and were still popular in the 1920s and 30s.

To present this music in the 1970s and 80s, many churches built brush arbors outside and others fashioned them inside over the choir. Gene and I wrote the title song for this collection and I think we were able to paint a word picture of that era. I hope as you read the words you will better understand just what a brush arbor meeting was and its impact on the people who participated:

> Listen, friends, and I'll tell you a story from sweet memories of sometime ago. A brush arbor shelter with God's air-conditioning where people loved to go. Rough wooden benches and kerosene lanterns and sawdust mixed with sand, our old brush arbor became a cathedral as we sang sweet "Beulah Land." I can remember the time when school was out and crops had all been laid by. People would gather at the old brush arbor to pray and testify. Old-time singing and old-time preaching could be heard for miles around, and voices singing the "Old-Time Religion" would bring such a heavenly sound.

Gene and I agreed on most of the lyrics for this tune but we had an argument over whether to say kerosene or coal-oil lantern. I won and we used *kerosene* because I thought the people might be more familiar with kerosene. However,

Gene had the last word, because at each performance he narrated he told about our argument and asked how many people knew what coal oil was. Hands would go up all over the audience.

4

Bach, Beethoven, Brahms, and Bartlett

In March, 1980, when Gene's retirement would officially begin, a testimonial luncheon was held at Trinity Baptist Church. It was billed as a "roast" and his friends did a good job. He was called "a seething volcano," the "Perry Como of Gospel Music," and a "shade-tree musician," among other names.

When the "roasting" was done, some made remarks which meant so much to Gene.

Dr. Joe L. Ingram, who was then executive director-treasurer of the Baptist General Convention of Oklahoma called Gene "one of the most influential persons among Oklahoma Baptists. Music is better in Oklahoma because of Gene, and we are grateful to him."

Leroy McClard of the Bapist Sunday School Board's Church Music Department in Nashville, Tennessee, said, "Music lovers all over the world recognize three great B's—Bach, Beethoven and Brahms. Southern Baptists recognize a fourth B—Bartlett."

The Singing Churchmen performed a medley of Gene's tunes and announced that they had elected him their "den mother," a phrase Gene had used to describe his role in arranging logistics for concerts and travel for the group.

John Gardner, also of the Sunday School Board who had

been a minister of music in Oklahoma, described Gene as a "shadetree musician." The phrase caught the imagination of Charles F. Brown, composer-publisher in Dallas, Texas. He later called Grace Hawthorne, a lyricist in Atlanta, Georgia, and told her about the luncheon and the description of Gene as a "shadetree musician." She asked if she could try to write some lyrics.

From this telephone call, Grace, Charlie, and Gene worked together on a musical for senior adults. "The Shadetree Musician" was published in 1983. It has a script and staging and makes a wonderful worship experience that also includes a children's choir at one point.

The song that pays tribute to Gene is entitled, "How Far a Life Can Reach." Here are the lyrics:

> From far away, you touched my life in ways you never knew, and from the start you made me feel that I was special too. I learned a lot of things from you, you never tried to teach and isn't it amazing just how far a life can reach? We never know the lives we touch as we go through each day, some laughter shared, some compliment, a prayer we thought to say; a word or two in sympathy becomes a noble speech, and isn't it amazing just how far a life can reach? I'll try to do for someone else what you have done for me, and that way what you had to give will live eternally. And that's the message Jesus taught each time He stopped to preach, and isn't it amazing just how far a life can reach?

5

Retirement's New Song

Even in retirement Gene continued to be interested in the small church and the untrained choir member.

It was with these in mind that he put together a collection of easy music for the revival choir. Published in 1983, it was titled "Thirty Minutes Early." The idea was that the music was simple enough that the revival choir could meet thirty minutes before the service was to begin, rehearse, and then sing for the evening service.

The collection included songs such as "I Want to Say a Word" in which Gene talks about the peace of Jesus Christ which is available to those who trust in Him and the witness Christians are to have as they say a word about Christ and share this love with others.

Julie Myers was our first grandchild. You know how grandfathers are about grandchildren, especially grand-daughters. Gene was no exception.

During the years Julie was growing up, we would make several trips each year to see my mother in Arkansas. When it was my turn to drive, Gene and Julie would get in the backseat of the car and write songs. From this beginning, "Fun Songs for Kids" by Paw Paw and Julie came to be published.

While I drove along, Gene would ask Julie about the things she liked to do. When she replied, "take a trip to the zoo" or "a trip to the country," they would write words about these events. They talked about God and church, about family, and the changing seasons.

When they had thirteen sets of lyrics written and Gene set them to tunes children could easily learn and sing. He sent them to Ralph Carmichael of Lexicon Music Co. Carmichael was enthusiastic about the project and decided that Gene and Julie would fly to California for the recording session. Ralph was going to find people to play Paw Paw and Julie.

When they arrived in California, it was determined that Julie would play herself and the voice of Paw Paw would be Thurl Ravenscroft (alias, "Tony the Tiger"). Julie was eight years old at this time.

Ralph Carmichael conducted the recording session. Children from the Hollywood area made up the choir. The musical adventure consisted of a record and songbook with pictures to color. The recording was especially good for teachers and children's workers.

After the recording session, Ralph Carmichael said, "I have never found so much happiness in a recording session before. I felt like Santa Claus at a Sunday School Christmas party."

The recording was done in 1975 and was the culmination of four years of work by Gene and Julie. She is now in her early twenties and, following studies at Oklahoma Baptist University, is pursuing a career in music.

After Gene's retirement, many churches continued to present his old-fashioned collections. He was invited to narrate and did quite a bit of traveling to help with the performances over the next three years.

He updated his overalls to a blue denim suit, but he continued to sit in the rocking chair and tell how a particular song came to be written. He shared what he remembered of the singing convention era. Usually the pastor joined him on the platform and together they reminisced about earlier days. These were happy times as the congregation was caught up in looking back and remembering.

During the many performances of the collections or services of Gene Bartlett music in cities from Florida to California, many wonderful worship experiences took place. There were renewals of commitments to Christ, mending of broken relationships, and strengthening of church families.

In one church two deacons who had been estranged for many years were present. They sat on opposite sides of the auditorium and each had his following in the church. During the invitation Gene stressed the importance of forgiving one another and renewing friendships as Christ had forgiven them.

The pastor later called Gene to tell him these two deacons had met after the service, prayed together, and forgave one another. He reported that a sweet, sweet Spirit now prevailed in the church.

In another church in California, the woman playing the piano for the service was able to renew fellowship with Christ. Several members of her family had been killed in a car accident the year before, including her parents. She felt great bitterness. As she played the old gospel songs that her parents had known and loved, the bitterness melted. Precious memories flooded over her that afternoon and she was able once again to feel God's love for her.

After an evening performance in a park in Arkansas, an elderly gentleman was present who had not spoken since suffering a stroke some months earlier. During the service he was able to talk about the old hymns and to share some of his memories as he sang along.

In Texas, a ninety-year-old man had expressed his happiness at hearing songs he never thought he'd hear again. "It was the best time I've had in years," he said. His family later told Gene that before they reached their car, he suffered a heart attack and died. They were rejoicing that he had been able to participate in the service.

I recall very vividly one night during a service seeing a man in his twenties come forward during the invitation. The entire congregation was in tears as another young man came out of the choir and they embraced at the altar. We learned later that they had been the best of friends during their early teens. Through a misunderstanding this relationship had been broken and their estrangement had severely affected the youth ministry of the church. There at the altar they received God's forgiveness and forgave each other. The bitterness and hatred melted away as they experienced a restored relationship. God's grace, so amazing, had been manifested once again.

In 1971 the executive board of the Southern Baptist Woman's Missionary Union was looking for a song for Acteens, young women thirteen-to-nineteen years old involved in mission study and action. Gene submitted a song, "This Is Our Day," which was selected to be the theme song for Southern Baptist Acteens. It was widely used and Gene was elated at the response of teenagers throughout the Convention. This enabled him once again to say something meaningful to the youth of our land whom he loved so much and who will be the leaders of our mission work tomorrow.

Today's Acteens do not know Gene as well as those who were around when the song was adopted. However, during a recent summer, as a group of Oklahoma Acteens learned the song at their camp, they were impressed that an adult had written their very own song and wrote letters expressing their appreciation to Gene. He cherished the letters from the girls and their sponsors.

Not long before Gene's death, Acteens at Portland Avenue Baptist Church in Oklahoma City dedicated their awards ceremony to him and he was able to attend. "This Is Our Day" was the theme for the evening. The girls had cross-stitched a picture for him and had also written their own stanza to the theme song for Gene. To be so loved and remembered was very thrilling.

Conclusion:
Life After Parkinson's

More than thirteen years after the diagnosis that Gene had Parkinson's disease, we could truly say, yes, there is life after Parkinson's.

The same God who was with us when we began the difficult journey with this disease in 1975 was with us at the end. Our lives took new directions since that day. We tried to live one day at a time. Sometimes we managed to do better at letting go and letting God direct our paths than at other times. But deep in our spirits, we knew that only He saw the whole picture, that He loved us, and that His plans for us were better than any we could imagine.

We prayed for God to heal Gene's body. That did not happen in the sense that we asked. Yet we knew that there were many times and types of healing. For example, there were many occasions when it would have been physically impossible for Gene to complete a project or perform a special task. My inclination often would have been to cancel the effort, but Gene's incredible faith in Christ would cause him to say, "Let's go ahead. I believe God will take over."

Gene would go ahead, God would take over, and the task would be completed. I saw this happen again and again.

Parkinson's is not a pretty disease, if *any* disease can be called that. For Gene, as for other victims, it took away his facial expressions and put a mask on his features. Gene lost a tremendous amount of weight in the last two years of his life. He also suffered from "lock-ups" when every bodily function slowed to a standstill. These began after prolonged use of available medications for the disease.

Gene's sense of humor often saved him from giving up. When a lock-up hit Gene, if he was walking, the only way he could continue moving was to speed up his pace to a slow jog. This happened once when Gene was walking down the corridor of a large Dallas hotel. An employee of the hotel spotted Gene and said, "Sir, you can't jog in the hotel." Gene kept going, knowing that to stop would be to fall down. The man repeated, "Sir! Sir! You can't jog in the hotel!" Gene kept moving but called back over his shoulder, "Sorry, I can't help it." About that time Gene's brother, Charles, came along and helped him to his room, but we laughed many times as we tried to imagine the thoughts of the hotel employee.

The disease sometimes caused Gene's mouth to form facial grimaces. One Sunday recently a little girl sitting in front of us at church kept watching him and after several efforts was able to hold her mouth exactly like his. Her mother was embarrassed, but we thought the child was pretty observant for a three-year old.

But even as we were forced to cope with the ravages of the disease, there also were countless blessings which reminded us of God's presence with us and brought joy to our lives.

For example, in August 1979 we received a piece of mail with "The White House" written on the outside of the envelope. There is a restaurant in Oklahoma by that name where Gene and I had celebrated our wedding anniversary the previous year. We assumed we had received an invitation to dine with them once again. Imagine our surprise upon opening the envelope to find an invitation from President and Mrs. Jimmy Carter inviting us to an old-fashioned gospel singing at the White House on Sunday afternoon, September 9, 1979. Of course, we attended. It was a beautiful time of gospel singing by country and gospel artists and we thoroughly enjoyed sitting on blankets, and eating fried chicken and banana pudding.

A funny sidelight occurred in connection with the event. A photographer from Baptist Press was going to take our picture and had been told to look for a couple sitting on an Indian blanket. The only problem was there were many couples sitting on a large number of Indian blankets.

In June 1984 we took a Mediterranean cruise to visit the Holy Land. Gene knew that I had longed to see the land where our Savior lived and walked. He said he thought he could manage a cruise.

One day our good friend Helen Riley saw a cruise advertised in the paper. We began to make inquiries and with Helen and her husband, Cleve, who had been our traveling companions many times, we decided to go. We knew that Gene would not be able to do everything on our schedule. However, he was able to participate in those things he was most interested in doing.

At every port of call, trips inland were planned and Gene was able to go to the ruins of Delphi and to Israel. When he stayed aboard ship, the crew took very good care of him.

On the day we visited the Parthenon in Athens, Gene remained at the hotel. He was returning to our room when he heard the cleaning women singing. He began to sing, "Jesus Loves Me," and they joined him.

Isn't it amazing how God manifests His love even when we are far from home?

In Israel it was especially significant to us to walk in the Garden of Gethsemane. We could imagine our Lord kneeling there to pray so long ago. We breathed a prayer of thanksgiving for His sacrifice.

Following Gene's retirement he was honored in special ways beyond anything he might think or imagine. We were careful to give God the praise.

In 1985 the Southern Baptist Church Music Conference honored Gene with the W. Hines Sims Award given to a church musician who has made an outstanding contribution to church music. The awards committee is very selective and the award is not given every year.

Gene was able to travel to Dallas for the presentation made by Dick Ham. He talked about Gene as a composer of songs. I think, however, Dick's words which were most meaningful to Gene that day were these:

"I think the best way to characterize Gene Bartlett is to say first of all that he is a man who loves people very, very much. He is also a man who is loved very, very much. The marvelous choral group who share this platform with me today are a result of Gene's dream. He is the founder of the Singing Churchmen of Oklahoma. So it is fitting and appropriate that we bestow this award on 'Uncle Gene,' Gene Bartlett. . . . Uncle Gene, we love you and are pleased to present this award to you today."

In September 1986 Trinity Baptist Church had a day of celebration for us. At that time plans were unveiled for a music suite at the church to be named the Gene and Emma-Jeanne Bartlett Music Suite. It was a wonderful time of celebration as friends and colleagues from across the convention came to pay tribute to a man and his music. Special highlights for Gene were a medley of his tunes arranged for and sung by the Singing Churchmen and the attendance of friends and former members of Trinity. Many had traveled hundreds of miles to help us celebrate.

The Church Music Department of the Baptist General Convention of Oklahoma is planning to build a carillon clock tower at Falls Creek to be called "The Bartlett Tower" in Gene's honor. It will be erected near the tabernacle and serve to call the young people to classes and to worship services. As the beautiful music rings out over the grounds of Falls Creek, it was Gene's prayer that it will serve to call the youth of our state to lives committed to Jesus Christ.

As the Parkinson's progressed, Gene could no longer sing and it was very difficult for him to write. This put an end to his composing, but the words and the tunes were still in his heart and mind.

And now, as Gene is with the Lord, I have every reason to believe that he is writing songs and, yes, leading a choir!